WALKING IN THE SOUTH WALES VALLEYS

About the Author

Mike Dunn was born and bred in the Midlands but has lived in Penarth, in the Vale of Glamorgan, for more than 25 years. He worked for the Welsh Assembly government, latterly specialising in environmental and conservation issues, and has written widely on landscape, walking, pubs and real ale. His books include *The Penguin Guide to Real Draught Beer*, *Walking Through the Lake District*, *Walking Ancient Trackways* and, most recently (and with Mick Slaughter), *Real Heritage Pubs of Wales*. Mike is married with two daughters and his interests include tennis, cricket, walking – especially in the Lake District, the Scottish Islands and Wales and the Welsh Borders – and good beer.

WALKING IN THE SOUTH WALES VALLEYS

by Mike Dunn

2 POLICE SQUARE, MILNTHORPE, CUMBRIA LA7 7PY
www.cicerone.co.uk

Printed by KHL Printing, Singapore

A catalogue record for this book is available from the British Library.
Photos © Chris & Mike Dunn 2012

Acknowledgements

Many people have provided help and inspiration while this book was researched
and written, but I would particularly like to thank three groups: the local authority rights of way officers in South Wales, especially Stacey Humber, Leigh Tuck,
Gwyn Teague, Owen Struthers and Andrew Fleming; those who provided specialist information on a variety of subjects – Guy Bradley, Phil and Gwenda Davies,
Howard Dukes, Daniel Jenkins-Jones, Janet Pedwell and Ivor Penberthy; and the
walkers, notably Huw Brodie and Chris, Kate and Sarah Dunn.

Advice to Readers

While every effort is made by our authors to ensure the accuracy of guide-
books as they go to print, changes can occur during the lifetime of an edi-
tion. If we know of any, there will be an Updates tab on this book's page on
the Cicerone website (www.cicerone.co.uk), so please check before planning your trip. We also advise that you check information about such things
as transport, accommodation and shops locally. Even rights of way can be
altered over time. We are always grateful for information about any discrep-
ancies between a guidebook and the facts on the ground, sent by email to
info@cicerone.co.uk or by post to Cicerone, 2 Police Square, Milnthorpe
LA7 7PY, United Kingdom.

Front cover: The Ogwr Fach valley and the Severn estuary from Craig Ogwr (Walk 12)

CONTENTS

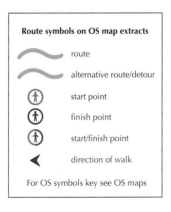

Approaching the summit plateau of Craig yr Allt (Walk 11, Stage 3)

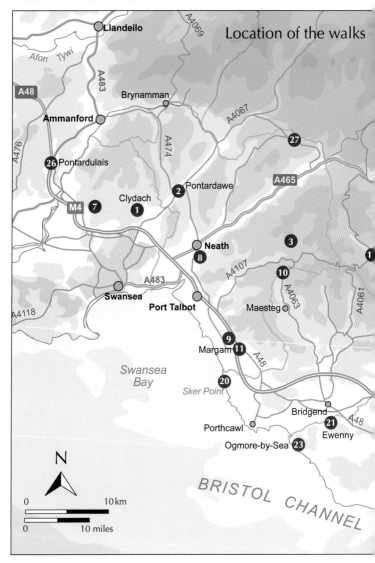

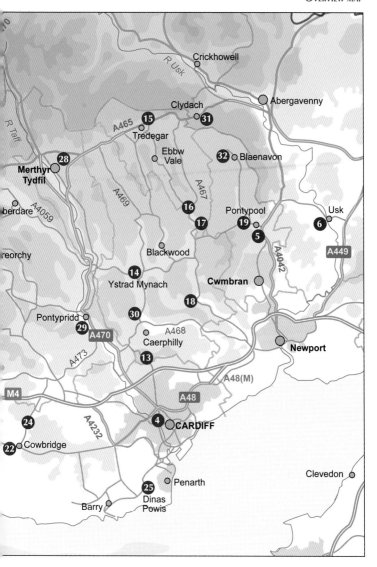

The Lower Clydach River at Forge Fach (Walk 1)

INTRODUCTION

The Usk Valley from the southern slopes of the Blorenge (Walk 32)

Soaring ridges separating deep, green valleys; spectacular and varied scenery; a rich heritage and a huge variety of walks all crammed into a compact, easily accessible region. Welcome to the South Wales valleys – a region reborn for the 21st century, yet still waiting to be discovered by discerning walkers.

The area offers extraordinary landscapes – the valleys, once ravaged by the industrial revolution, are now almost totally reclaimed, and the uplands between them are green and fresh, having been practically untouched. The transition from valley to upland is astonishingly sudden: tracks lead out of the urban valley floors and within a few steps a rural landscape beckons, with craggy, wooded valley sides, heather moors and classic views of houses clinging to steep hillsides and pastoral scenes with distant mountains.

This is truly a layered landscape. The paths and tracks are littered with reminders of the people who have walked these routes before – Celtic saints, Roman soldiers, medieval packhorse trains, Methodist lay preachers and ironminers among them. It is a shared landscape, too.

The walker often feels privileged to roam in the company of other creatures, from foxes patrolling the Sarn Helen Roman road and brown hares on the Coed Morgannwg plateau, to birds of prey soaring above the moorlands and forests. At times, the landscape is expansive, with astonishing panoramas northwards to the peaks of the Brecon Beacons, or southwards across the Severn Estuary to the Somerset and Devon hills. At times, it is intimate, with hidden chapels, secluded side valleys and forgotten heritage.

To many, South Wales is a region of industrial grime, black coal and grey factories. This perception is wrong – only the flat valley floors succumbed to the embrace of the industrial revolution and its collieries, ironworks and mounds of waste material. Terraced housing often sits alongside or perches at improbable angles on the lower slopes but the uplands were virtually untouched. The gently sloping moorland summits continue to sustain ancient sheepwalks, while the wooded slopes beneath them were too steep to be exploited.

Now, the collieries and ironworks have either been swept away or reinvented as tourist destinations, and the spoil heaps landscaped or removed. In fact, all preconceptions should be firmly left behind in order to savour the unexpected – the castellated round towers at Nantyglo, the grottos at Abercregan, the mysterious Strawberry Wall at Ynysybwl – and

revel in the delightful walking available in this green and uncrowded area.

The industrial past of the area works in favour of present-day walkers. The railways, tramroads and canal towpaths that sustained industry now provide superb pedestrian walkways, reaching parts that are sometimes inaccessible to other, more ancient, rights of way. The tramroads around Blaenavon and the Clydach Gorge, for example, are easy to follow, a delight to walk, and are set in the sensational scenery of the Brecon Beacons National Park, while canal towpaths thread their way through several of the valleys.

Sandwiched between the Loughor Valley to the west and the Vale of Usk to the east, the Brecon Beacons to the north and the Severn Estuary to the south, this is a land of contrasts: from rolling hills to deep valleys, remote moorland to coastal lowlands, with huge areas of sand dunes and pristine beaches. As a consequence, there is a huge variety of walking available, ranging from challenging ridgetop routes and spectacular cliff edge paths, to idyllic, gentle valley strolls.

GEOLOGY AND LANDSCAPE

Geologically, South Wales is a remarkably young landscape: its oldest rocks are around only 400 million years old, compared with the Precambrian rocks of Pembrokeshire, which are several hundred million years older. The landscape of the valleys and the coastal plain reflects this to some extent, although it has also been strongly influenced by much more recent geological processes, particularly the events at the end of the last Ice Age, a mere 10,000 or so years ago.

The geological story of the valleys also includes successive periods of mountain building, including the Silurian period (400 million years ago) and the Variscan orogeny (100 million years later), represented by the Triassic sandstones and mudstones of the Vale of Glamorgan. These periods were interspersed with episodes of large-scale deposition, including the intervening Devonian period, during which a 2000m-thick layer of sandstone, mudstone and conglomerates was laid down.

At the end of the Devonian period, the river plains of South Wales were flooded by a shallow sea, which resulted in the deposition of fossil-rich carboniferous limestones. The Upper Carboniferous rocks were to have a massive influence 350 million years later: within them was a layer of peat deposits that was later buried and compressed to form coal seams up to 1800m thick – seams that were central to the role that Wales played in the 19th century as the powerhouse of the Industrial revolution.

The next key development in the geological history of the South Wales valleys was a further episode of flooding. The area lay under a fairly shallow and warm sea, which deposited Jurassic limestones and mudstones. These are a familiar sight along the Glamorgan Heritage Coast, with their wave-cut platforms, stacks, caves and dry valleys.

A Pennant Sandstone quarry east of Bryn (Walk 9, Stage 1)

Rocks younger than these are almost entirely absent from the region, having been eroded away. The period during which the rocks were uplifted and contorted had important consequences: the development of cave systems and other karst features in the carboniferous limestones, together with folding and faulting in the coal measures. This later led to difficulties in extracting coal and the subsequent closure on geological grounds of many of the coal mines.

All this mountain building, deposition and erosion has had a huge effect on the landscape, but arguably more important still are the events of the last two million years, including a series of Ice Ages. The most severe was around 20,000 years ago when almost all Wales lay beneath ice sheets. Gradual warming that started 18,000 years ago led to a rise in sea level, the formation of over-deepened valleys as meltwater gouged out new channels, and the masking of older rock formations under a thin layer of drift deposits.

The result of all this activity is a richly varied landscape, including the deeply dissected plateau of the valleys, with broad mountain ridges riven by a series of deeply entrenched valleys running roughly north to south, the lower plateau of the Vale of Glamorgan and its abrupt ending at the cliffs of the Heritage Coast, and the estuaries and lowlands around Kenfig, Ogmore, Cardiff and Newport. The changes are, of course, still in progress, not least in this coastal zone, where rockfalls and other erosive activities are still common, and where the deposition of wind-blown sand overwhelmed whole towns in the medieval period.

Nash Point and the overdeepened valley of Cwm Marcross (Walk 23)

PLANTS AND WILDLIFE

The legacy of this remarkably varied landscape, and especially of the dissected plateau, with its intricate mosaic of mountain and valley in close proximity, is seen in the huge variety of habitats present in a relatively small area, and therefore in the diversity of plants and wildlife that can be enjoyed in the course of relatively short walks in the region.

As late as the early 20th century, traditional farming practices persisted in rural South Wales, with colourful meadows, pasture land and small arable fields, all divided by flourishing hedgerows. Changes in farming practices spelled the end for many of the hedges, with larger fields proving to be more productive as a result of the use of herbicides and pesticides, but at the cost of a massive reduction in diversity and colour. Hay meadows are rare now, while there has been an enormous decline in wild flowers such as cowslips (once common in field margins) and most species of farmland birds. Nature reserves often provide

(Clockwise from top left): wigeon at Cosmeston Lakes (Walk 25); yellowhammer near St Brides Major (Walk 21); stonechat at Capel Newydd (Walk 19); kestrel hovering above the Heritage Coast path (Walk 23)

A red admiral at the Upper Lliw reservoir (Walk 7)

Pearly everlasting thriving by Sarn Helen (Walk 27)

the last refuge for formerly common birds, although there are welcome surprises. Yellowhammers thrive in oilseed rape near the Heritage Coast, and butterflies such as the familiar red admiral and more exotic comma survive in suitable habitat throughout the lowlands.

Change is just as apparent at higher levels, with large tracts of heather moorland swept away by a combination of pressures including the intensification of farming, the setting of fires and extensive afforestation. Only on the Blorenge and in one or two other places is there sufficient heather for the red grouse to flourish. Elsewhere, a mosaic of bilberry, gorse and coarse grasses and sedge vegetation support populations of ground-nesting birds such as meadow pipits and skylarks, the latter with their delightful liquid song, together with pink-breasted, white-rumped

wheatears. This is also the territory of many of Wales's birds of prey, including buzzards, kestrels and, increasingly, red kites. Other raptors such as merlins, hobbies and goshawks also patrol the skies here but are much less likely to be seen.

Native woodland clings on, often on the lower valley sides. Sessile oaks are a major feature of the surviving ancient woodlands in the valleys, but better still are the beechwoods, which thrive on the limestone rim of the South Wales coalfield, along the ridge north of Cardiff and especially in the Clydach Gorge, west of Abergavenny. Even colliery waste provides a suitable habitat for specialist plants such as pearly everlasting (*anaphalis margaritacea*), which is particularly abundant on coal tips in Glamorgan and Monmouthshire.

On the higher slopes, conifer plantations once dominated the landscape, but many of the forests have reached maturity and large areas have been clear-felled. It is now popular to allow natural regeneration or, where the original plantations were relatively unsuccessful, to revert to open land, so that the views are now the most extensive they have been for decades. The remaining plantations provide a refuge for pine martens and deer and a habitat for crossbills, siskins and coal tits, while recent clearfell is favoured by the elusive nightjar.

Water features bring additional variety to the scene, with birds such as dippers, grey wagtails and kingfishers in the cleaner rivers, and shoreweed, lobelia and floating burweed in the lakes, where common sandpipers may be seen alongside mallard, teal, coot and grebes. Disappointingly, many of the upland lakes are bird-free. Canals mimic rivers in some ways but also provide a specialist habitat for plants rare to the area, such as lesser water-parsnip and arrowhead, and for a variety of fish. The Glamorgan coastline is home to chough, rock pipits and other shore birds, and an impressive variety of seabirds during spring and autumn migrations.

THE IMPACT OF MAN

The human landscape of the lowlands is astonishingly young. Almost everything from before the late 18th century was sacrificed to the needs of the industrial revolution. The flat land in the valley floors was used for coal and iron works and for transport links. In the uplands, however, things are very different. A burial cairn here, a hillfort there, traces of medieval house platforms across the valley; the landscape is peppered with evidence of the use and re-use of moorland and farmland, with each successive wave of settlers modifying the landscape but unable (or unwilling) to obliterate completely the traces of their predecessors.

However, even in the uplands, the presence of early man can be glimpsed only through the scattered monuments that have survived, rather than through evidence of daily life in prehistoric times. Burial mounds, such as Carn Fach in Coed Morgannwg, together with cairn circles, notably the extraordinary Carn Llechart in the hills north of Swansea, give some insight into the way in which the dead were honoured. The most impressive monuments to survive are the Iron Age hillforts which guarded key routeways, including Caerau, Maendy Camp and Craig Ruperra.

The legacy of the Romans is easier to discern, although their interest in South Wales appears to have been fairly limited once they had established military control. The main Roman road through the area, the Via Julia Maritima, or Portway, from Caerleon near Newport through Cardiff and Neath and onwards to Carmarthen, has largely been reused in later times and evidence of its Roman origins is scarce. More minor roads such as Sarn Helen, which

The Carn Llechart ring cairn above Pontardawe (Walk 26)

ran north-eastwards from Neath to Coelbren and Brecon Gaer, can be traced much more easily in the landscape. Remains of the agger (earthwork), together with a Roman fortlet, are visible on the long ridge of Hirfynydd, while the ramparts of the fort at Coelbren also survive.

On the other side of the Neath Valley, an enormous marching camp is visible at Blaen Cwm-bach. Evidence of economic exploitation is much more limited, although there was farming around villas in the fertile Vale of Glamorgan, and Roman lead mines have been discovered at Draethen, in the Rhymney Valley.

The landscape evidence for man's activities over the centuries following the collapse of Roman rule is sketchy, with one or two spectacular surviving monuments masking a lack of real evidence of human impact. However, there is placename evidence for missionaries such as St Illtyd arriving from France and Ireland, and early religious cells were established at Llantwit Major and elsewhere.

Perhaps the most impressive features from this period, however, are the cross dykes, which were constructed in the eighth and ninth centuries to control movement along the high trackways used for long-distance travel. Excellent examples include Ffos Toncenglau at the head of the Rhondda Valleys, thrown up across the ancient trackway of Cefn Ffordd (now used by the Coed Morgannwg Way), and the cross dyke at Rhyd Blaen y Cwm on Mynydd Margam, close to the large Iron Age fort of Y Bwlwarcau above Llangynwyd, which may well have been reused during this period.

The imprint of the Normans on the South Wales landscape following their conquest of the area in the final years of the 11th century is a great deal easier to find. This can be seen largely through their network of castles, designed to emphasise the power and wealth of the new rulers and also of those local Welsh chieftains who were prepared to recognise Norman primacy and were rewarded with their own estates, particularly in the uplands. Norman castles controlled river crossing points and strategic military sites such as Neath, Kenfig, Ogmore and Cardiff. Many were relatively compact and some may have had a greater symbolic than defensive role, but at Caerphilly the Normans constructed one of the most spectacular castles in Europe.

A side effect of the Norman invasion was the foundation of monasteries, endowed with lands by the Norman conquerors and quick to introduce systems of land management, which changed the face of the Welsh agricultural landscape in ways that can still be recognised today. The Benedictines at Ewenny, and the Cistercians at Neath, Margam and Llantarnam amassed large estates and established grange farms to organise their agricultural activities. By the 13th century, Neath Abbey was exporting wool to Flanders and had more than a thousand acres of arable land at its grange at Monknash alone.

Villages in the lowlands were generally compact, with houses clustered around the church, while in the uplands a more scattered

The ruins of Margam Abbey (Walk 9, Stage 1)

pattern of settlement was favoured. This extended to summer dwellings for shepherds on the high moorland, and the remains of 'platform houses' can still be discovered today, mostly medieval in origin and consisting of two rooms, one for the farmer's family and one for the animals. Some were associated with monastic land management, including those on Mynydd Ty-talwyn on the Glamorgan Ridgeway. Parkland was rare until the dissolution of the monasteries paved the way for the creation of large estates, with deer parks enclosed at Margam and Ewenny, as well as St Donats and Caerphilly, where the deer park was enclosed within the Senghenydd Dyke in 1578.

INDUSTRY AND RELIGION

The landscape of the valleys was still heavily wooded until the onset of the industrial revolution, which saw whole hillsides stripped of trees in order to obtain the charcoal required for iron smelting. Worse still, the valleys and hill slopes were increasingly tarnished by the tipping of industrial waste from the ironworks and the collieries that sprang up to service them when coal was discovered to be superior to wood for smelting purposes. Merthyr Tydfil grew quickly from a small village to become a world-renowned industrial centre following the installation of the first furnace at Cyfarthfa in 1765. Its output was prodigious, but at the cost of exploitation,

both of working families and of the environment, which became blackened and barren.

At the same time, the valleys experienced a transport revolution. Canals, mostly constructed at breakneck speed in the 1790s, were often linked to tramroads and plateways. These were followed by the construction of a dense network of competing railways, designed to ferry the output of the forges and furnaces to the newly developed docks at Barry, Cardiff, Newport and elsewhere. Space in the flat valley floors was at a premium, so the familiar terraces of housing for the rapidly growing workforce occupied the lower slopes, often rising at crazy angles as the industrial towns snaked along the main valleys.

In 1775, William Edwards' newly constructed bridge over the River Taff at Pontypridd was described as 'environed on all sides by woody hills, cornfields, most luxuriant trees and some neat cottages'. Not for long. Although the higher land remained largely untouched, the valleys themselves had changed beyond recognition by 1854, when George Borrow undertook his tour of Wild Wales and described the pandemonium of 'immense stacks of chimneys surrounded by diabolical-looking buildings, in the neighbourhood of which were huge heaps of cinders and black rubbish'. From the chimneys, 'smoke was proceeding in volumes, choking the atmosphere all around'. It would be the second half of the

One of the furnaces at Blaenavon ironworks (Walk 32)

20th century before this exploitation of the natural landscape was decisively reversed.

Industrialisation and urbanisation was accompanied by a religious revival, led by the major nonconformist groups, including Calvinistic Methodists and Wesleyans. In the late 18th century, dissenters faced disapproval and their chapels were often hidden away – for example, Baran and Gerazim chapels in upland Gower, and Gyfylchi, high above the Afan Valley. By 1900, there were 150 chapels seating 85,000 people in the Rhondda Valleys alone – three seats for every four people living in the valley. Now, many of the chapels are redundant or have been converted to other uses, although they remain an important feature of the landscape.

GREENING THE VALLEYS

In the 19th century, South Wales provided one of the earliest industrial landscapes – although even then large swathes survived unscathed because industrial activity was largely confined to the valley floors and lower slopes. Now, the area's transformation to a green, vibrant and largely postindustrial landscape has almost been completed.

It has taken half a century and required exceptional vision, a significant injection of cash and a lot of blood, sweat and tears (not least those shed following the Aberfan disaster in 1966, which cost 144 lives, 116 of them children), but the outcome is startling. The coal mines are closed, virtually all traces swept away, except where they have been conserved as heritage attractions, such as the Big Pit in Blaenavon. They have been replaced by reclaimed and, in many cases, eye-catching landscapes – country parks, such as those in the Dare Valley and Parc Cwm Darren, and forest parks, including the internationally renowned mountain biking centres at Cwmcarn and Afan Forest Park.

The Aberfan disaster, caused when a waste tip slid down the mountainside above the village, engulfing a farm cottage, 20 houses, and Pantglas Junior School, provided the impetus for a sustained land reclamation programme that was breathtaking in its scale and longevity. Originally driven by the political imperative of ensuring the safety of the remaining waste tips, the programme evolved into a spur for the economic regeneration of the chronically disadvantaged valleys, before finding a further expression as a purely environmental programme aimed at improving health and quality of life through the provision of green spaces and recreation opportunities.

Incredibly, the programme has yet to reach a conclusion – the Ffos y Fran scheme on an old opencast coal mining site east of Merthyr Tydfil is unlikely to be completed until 2025 – but huge areas of colliery spoil have been removed or landscaped and major environmental successes have been achieved. At Llanilid, near Bridgend, for example, a vast opencast site has been replaced by woodland, open space and a network of footpaths. The area is now one of the best in South Wales for owls, including the rare short-eared owl, and raptors such

The restored Marine Colliery tip at Manmoel (Walk 15)

as the marsh harrier. Rivers have also been dramatically improved: once so polluted that no fish could survive, rivers such as the Afan and Taff now have thriving salmon populations.

The final element of this transformation from scarred landscape to environmental asset is the Valleys Regional Park, promoted by a consortium of public and voluntary bodies and aimed at completing the greening of the valleys, while improving public access still further. Several of the walks in this guide explore parts of the Regional Park.

THE WELSH LANGUAGE

While it is unlikely that you will hear much Welsh spoken – in preparing this guide I heard it only twice, in the surprisingly secluded hills north of Swansea – it is important to recognise that Welsh remains very much the language of the landscape, from *mynydd* for mountain to *cwm* for valley. Walking in the valleys and uplands of South Wales is therefore much more enjoyable if a few key words and phrases on the maps can be recognised to aid in interpreting the landscape.

To start at the top, *mynydd* translates as mountain, although this may sometimes apply to a summit as well as to a broader upland mass. There is no hard-and-fast distinction between mountain and hill, and *bryn*, *twyn* or *garth* may all signify either. A ridge may be denoted by *cefn* or, rarely in South Wales, *esgair*. *Rhiw* may also mean hill, but can also denote a slope, while a really steep slope is a *craig*.

Cwm Nant-gwyn and the Llynfi Valley (Walk 11, Stage 1)

23

A little lower, *rhos*, *waun* or *gwaun* may all relate to moorland, while *coed* means a wood and *allt* generally means wooded. Features that may be encountered in the landscape here or on the mountain tops include *carn* or *carnedd* (cairn), *caer* (fort), *sarn* (ancient road or causeway), *clawdd* (ditch, dyke or hedge), *llyn* (lake), and *ffynnon* (spring or well).

In the valley (variously *cwm*, *dyffryn*, *glyn*, *pant* or *ystrad*), a stream (*nant*) will form at its head (*blaen*), just below the *bwlch* or col, which separates it from a neighbouring valley, and may in due course become a river or *afon*. *Cymer* indicates a confluence of streams, while *aber* is the point at which a river joins a larger one – Aberdare, where the *Afon Dar* joins the *Afon Cynon*, for example – or where it reaches the sea, as with the *Afon Tawe* at Abertawe (Swansea).

Within the valley, some of the main features include *llan* (village, church or enclosure), *eglwys* (church) or *capel* (chapel), *ty* (house), *plas* (mansion), *heol* or *ffordd* (road), *pont* (bridge), *rhyd* (ford), *ynys* (island), *melin* (mill), and *cae* or *maes* (field).

A further difficulty is mutation, through which the initial letter of a word may change depending on the word it follows, usually in order to help with pronunciation, so that 'in Cardiff (*Caerdydd*)' is rendered as '*yng Nghaerdydd*'. Fortunately, place names on maps are rarely affected by this convention!

GETTING TO AND AROUND SOUTH WALES

Newport, Cardiff, Bridgend and Swansea are the main transport hubs for walkers in the South Wales valleys. All are on the inter-city route from London Paddington to South and West Wales, with frequent, fast services seven days a week. The same centres are served by trains from Manchester, while Newport and Cardiff also have direct services from Bristol, Exeter and the South Coast, Birmingham, Nottingham and North Wales.

The Rhondda, Cynon, Taff, Rhymney and Ebbw valleys have good rail connections to Cardiff, while the western valleys (and others such as the Sirhowy) rely on often surprisingly good bus services to nearby urban centres. A dense network of local bus services, including some that run remarkably frequently, proves very useful in a number of places in completing the walks described in this guide. A summary of relevant services is given in the introduction to each walk, but the good news is that every walk in this book can be accessed by regular public transport services. Check the comprehensive Traveline Cymru website (www.traveline-cymru.info) for full details of services or call them on 0871 200 22 33 (7am to 10pm, calls cost 10p a minute).

The valleys also have an exceptional network of cycle paths, often making use of the trackbed of disused railways, whose main economic

The Cymbyr Bridge over the Monmouthshire Canal is on a Sustrans cycle route (Walk 18)

purpose is long gone. For those who want to combine cycling with walking, they constitute an alternative, traffic-free means of reaching the start of many of the walks.

If you wish to extend your time in South Wales, there is a huge range of hotel, guest house, self-catering, hostel and campsite accommodation available. Suggestions have been made for overnight stops on the two multi-stage routes in this guide (Walk 9 and Walk 11) but otherwise your best bet for the latest information is to check the Visit Wales website (www.visitwales.co.uk) and search by area, or call the Visit Wales Contact Centre on 08708 300 306 (9am to 5pm, Mon to Fri) to find somewhere to base yourself.

There are also tourist information offices in Blaenavon (01495 742333), Bridgend (01656 654906), Caerphilly (029 2088 0011), Cardiff (029 2087 3573), Merthyr Tydfil (01685 727474), Swansea (01792 468321) and Porthcawl (01656 786639) who will be able to offer advice.

WHAT TO TAKE

A well-stocked rucksack in South Wales will inevitably include decent waterproofs, for the weather can change quite quickly and, given the region's position in south-western Britain, there is always the chance of rain. That said, gloriously sunny days are equally possible and the weather is rarely extreme. Spare warm clothes

25

Casual moorings on the popular towpath near Ty Aur (Walk 5)

are always worth carrying, and the area's heritage, coupled with some superb viewpoints, make a camera essential, together with binoculars to spot the local wildlife.

None of the routes cover particularly arduous terrain and a pair of lightweight walking boots should survive any of them. There is a dense network of restricted byways, bridleways and footpaths, augmented by canal towpaths and walking routes created on the huge number of abandoned railway lines. Vast areas of the uplands have been designated as open access land, with the freedom to roam at will.

MAPS AND WAYMARKING

Maps, compass and (especially in woodland) a GPS should always be carried. The whole of the area is covered in six 1:25,000 Ordnance Survey maps:

- Outdoor Leisure 12 (Brecon Beacons – west and central areas)
- Outdoor Leisure 13 (Brecon Beacons – eastern area)
- Explorer 151 (Cardiff & Bridgend)
- Explorer 152 (Newport & Pontypool)
- Explorer 165 (Swansea)
- Explorer 166 (Rhondda & Merthyr Tydfil)

Waymarking is variable, but improving. There are some examples of best practice, but some routes need additional signposting to remove potential difficulties with route-finding. In these cases, a more detailed description of the way to overcome the difficulties is given in the text.

USING THIS GUIDE

There are 32 walks in the guide, a number of which are relatively short excursions that can be completed comfortably in half a day, while others are relatively challenging all-day expeditions that require rather more careful planning and a good level of fitness. Two, the Coed Morgannwg Way, a well-established challenge trail in the western valleys, and the Glamorgan Ridgeway, running east-west across the ridges rising above the Vale of Glamorgan, have been split into stages.

The walks are described in five sections, covering the valleys themselves, the western and eastern ridges, the Vale of Glamorgan and its coastline, and walks that explore aspects of the fascinating history and heritage of the area. Part 1 explores some of the rivers and canals of the area, following part of the well-known Taff Trail but also seeking out hidden gems such as the painstakingly restored Swansea Canal and the Cwm Cregan Trail. Parts 2 and 3 explore the western and eastern ridges, respectively, generally using well-defined ridgeway routes with spectacular views. Part 4 focuses on the lowlands around Bridgend and the Vale of Glamorgan, including a magnificent section of the Glamorgan Heritage Coast and a walk

centred on a town buried under sand in late medieval times. Part 5 provides a selection of routes exploring the rich and varied history of the area, tracing part of the Sarn Helen Roman road, following a pilgrimage route to the shrine of the Virgin Mary above the Rhondda Valleys and the medieval deer park wall of Senghenydd Dyke, and unearthing the industrial heritage of the Clydach Gorge and the Blaenavon World Heritage Site.

Each walk follows a common format, including a route introduction, which summarises the type of walk and the landscape and historical highlights encountered along the way. There is a route information box, including the start and finish points; the distance in miles and kilometres; the total ascent in metres and feet; the OS Explorer map(s) required to follow the route in detail; and information on the public transport available at each end of the walk, with an emphasis on the services needed to get you back to the start of the walk. In almost every case, this is sufficiently good that, even if the walk is not a circular one, it can be completed without the need for two cars or other special arrangements.

The time needed to complete the walks will obviously vary quite widely with the fitness, experience and in some cases age of the participants. Formulae do exist to convert distance and ascent into timings, but as a rough rule of thumb a party of average ability should be able to cover around two miles an hour, including stops to

The Afan Valley from above Cynonville (Walk 9, Stage 1)

investigate points of interest encountered during the walk. Approximate timings have been given for each route in this guide on this basis.

Each walk is then described in detail, with cross-referencing to the OS map extract provided and particular attention paid to points along the route where the path to be followed is not altogether obvious. Finally, the description also includes notes on features of historical or natural interest on or very close to the walk.

1 THE VALLEYS

The descent to Trebanos from below Eithrim (Walk 1)

WALK 1
Cwm Clydach and the Swansea Canal

Start/Finish	RSPB Cwm Clydach reserve, Lone Lane, Clydach (SS 683 026)
Distance	8 miles (13km)
Ascent	200m (655ft)
Time	3–4hrs
Map(s)	Explorer 165
Public transport	Bus 121 from Swansea to Craig Cefn Parc (hourly) passes the entrance to the RSPB reserve.

The undoubted highlight of this walk is the RSPB's Cwm Clydach reserve, a delightful area of ancient deciduous woodland alongside the Lower Clydach River. There is also an attractive bridge at Pont Llechart, the lonely Unitarian chapel on the slopes of Mynydd Gellionnen, and the return to Clydach along the towpath of the Swansea Canal, largely disused since the 1930s but now recognised as a valuable leisure resource.

Start at the southern tip of the long and sinuous RSPB reserve, which occupies the deep, well-wooded valley of the Lower Clydach River. Take the wooded riverside path, crossing at the second bridge and turning left on to the Trussler Trail. The path becomes quite rough, eventually climbing away from the river to reach a bridleway just south of Ty-llwydyn Farm. Turn left here, following the lane to a junction a little way above Pont Llechart. ◀

Drop down to inspect the sturdy bridge at Pont Llechart; there is room for a picnic beside the bridge, where the rushing water of the Nant Llwydyn joins the main river. Cross the bridge and take the minor road as it climbs eastwards, winding through woodland and then running along the edge of **Mynydd Gellionnen**, an area of classic flat upland common, grazed by both sheep and cattle. There are excellent views here across Cwm Clydach to the whale-backed hill of Mynydd Gelliwastad, an attractive area of common land with heather, bilberry

The bird life is stunning: dippers and grey wagtail frequent the river, pied flycatchers and redpoll dart among the trees, and buzzards and, increasingly, red kites can be seen and heard overhead.

The classic upland common of Mynydd Gellionnen

and some woodland. On reaching the plateau, a bridle-way leaves the road to the right. Take this broad, rutted track to arrive at the isolated Gellionnen

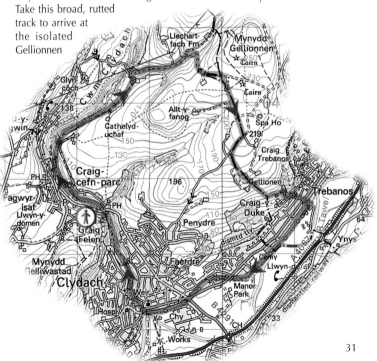

31

Chapel in its remarkable setting on the edge of the common.

Gellionnen Chapel, often called the 'white chapel', was built in 1692 by Protestant dissenters at the junction of the old roads from Swansea to Brecon, and Ammanford to Neath. It was rebuilt in 1801, with the ancient Gellionnen Stone incorporated into the wall. The original stone is now in Swansea Museum, with a copy inserted into the chapel wall. The chapel has suffered because of its isolated position: astonishingly, its historic interior was attacked by vandals in 2008 and it is now being painstakingly restored by the congregation.

Follow the track – waterlogged at times – across the common, which has superb all-round vistas. Pass above the farmhouse of Eithrim (named after an 11th-century Catholic church that was built nearby on the site of a Celtic holy place) and reach the road at the south-west edge of the common. Turn right along the road, then left along a bridleway, which begins as a farm access road but becomes a green lane, descending between hedges.

For a while the going is rough, across exposed bedrock at times, but the path then contours along the hillside, before meeting a tarmac lane at a gate. Descend steeply as the lane enters the suburban village of **Trebanos**. Go straight across the main road by the Colliers Arms pub to reach the Swansea Canal on its sylvan shelf above the River Tawe.

Built between 1784 and 1798, the **Swansea Canal** ran for 16 miles (25.5km) to its terminus at Abercraf, rising some 115m by way of 36 locks. Its key role was to transport coal, iron and steel from the upper Tawe Valley to Swansea docks, but its prosperity was short-lived and the upper reaches of the canal were abandoned by the end of the 19th century. The canal remained open as far as Clydach until 1931, and was largely forgotten, except as a source

of water for local industry, until its rebirth as a recreational resource.

The Swansea Canal north of Clydach

Turn right alongside the canal and follow it southwards towards Swansea, initially along a narrow tarmac lane as the canal descends through two disused locks. The lock gates have been removed and replaced by little cascades but the collar and anchor straps of the bottom gates of the upper lock are still there. What follows is a delightful stretch of canal, with tall trees to the right and the flat floor of the Tawe Valley to the left. Later, the Tawe runs very close as the path follows a narrow causeway between the canal and river.

As the canal veers away from the river there is an attractive stretch through deciduous trees, running alongside a golf course and a park, and then under a dark road bridge. At this point the towpath has a suburban feel, which is enhanced when the canal suddenly disappears into a culvert and for 200m the path is diverted around an industrial site. Just as suddenly, the canal reappears and the towpath makes for **Clydach** Lock, crosses the B4291 and rounds a factory to arrive at the aqueduct which carries the canal impressively over the Lower Clydach River just before its confluence with the Tawe.

Cross the canal on the footbridge just before the aqueduct, turn left to reach the main road and take the riverside footpath on the far side, following the Lower Clydach River back to the start of the walk. The river can be seen tumbling down a rock barrier at Forge Fach, with an excellent leat leading from above the cascades to the old forge site. Finally, the path runs between riverside woodland and steep sandstone cliffs to arrive at the entrance to the reserve.

WALK 2

Along the Tawe Valley

Start	Pontardawe (SN 721 040)
Finish	Ystalyfera (SN 771 090)
Distance	5½ miles (9km)
Ascent	Negligible
Time	2–3hrs
Map(s)	Explorer 165
Public transport	There is a service at least every hour on buses X20 and X25 from Swansea to both Pontardawe and Ystalyfera.

Fascinating remains of the higher reaches of the Swansea Canal (the last of the major Welsh canals, completed in 1798) lend extra interest to this gentle towpath and riverside walk. Several lock chambers can be seen, and in addition there is the abandoned branch canal leading to the ironworks at Ynyscedwyn – parts of which still stand – and an impressive aqueduct at Gurnos, near the end of the walk in Ystalyfera.

Start in Herbert Street in **Pontardawe** town centre, first going slightly south to see the canal crossing the Upper Clydach River on an aqueduct and then heading north past the parish church with its remarkably slender spire.

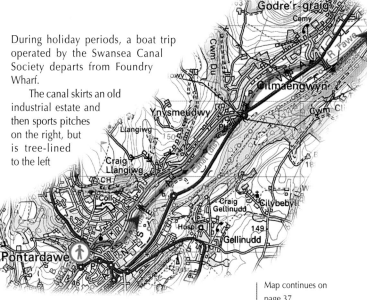

During holiday periods, a boat trip operated by the Swansea Canal Society departs from Foundry Wharf.

The canal skirts an old industrial estate and then sports pitches on the right, but is tree-lined to the left

Map continues on page 37

as it reaches open country at bridge 7. Here, St Illtyd's Walk, with its black and yellow waymarks, comes in from the left and follows the towpath for some 1¾ miles (3km). Beyond bridge 8, where a path leads up to Craig Llangiwg, a bit of detective work will uncover the remains of the Cilybebyll arm of the canal, which served a number of local collieries, as an overgrown trench heading east from the main line.

The towpath continues northwards along the pleasantly tree-lined canal to **Ynysmeudwy**, reaching locks 12 and 13, bereft of lock gates but still a fascinating sight. ▸

Above the locks the canal curves gently left, passing under an accommodation bridge and then a small, stone-built aqueduct over a stream before reaching the road at **Cilmaengwyn**. The road bridge here has been reconstructed and there is now no clearance for the towpath.

Beyond the road bridge the width of the canal is severely reduced by encroaching vegetation as it passes through a local nature reserve, but the towpath follows the narrow water channel past lock 14 at Cwm-tawe-isaf. ▸

At the lower of the two locks a lengthman's hut survives, together with a cast-iron support for the unique style of paddle gearing that was used on this canal.

The wrought-iron rings enclosing the heel post or pivot of one of the decaying lower lock gates still survive.

It then ends abruptly at the Swansea Valley road, the A4067. The route of the canal can be discerned all the way to Ystalyfera, but the remains are discontinuous and hard to follow in places, so instead cross the busy A4067 with care, walk left along the verge for 100m and then take a track that heads down to a footbridge over the River Tawe. The views north to the stepped cliffs of Varteg Hill are particularly impressive from here, while straight ahead is a farm at Tareni Gleision, which is surrounded by forested slopes dotted with abandoned mines and levels – and Gleision Colliery, the site of a tragic accident in 2011.

Climb up slightly to join the Cwm Tawe cycleway on its disused railway line; after just over half a mile (1km) there is a choice between following the cycleway all the way to the river crossing just south of Ystalyfera (an easy but not particularly interesting stroll) or branching left to follow a path along the river bank, passing a weir and rapids and eventually passing under the river crossing. From here, the paths unite, hugging the river bank under Darren Fach, with its crags and spoil heaps, and then

The River Tawe below Darren Fach

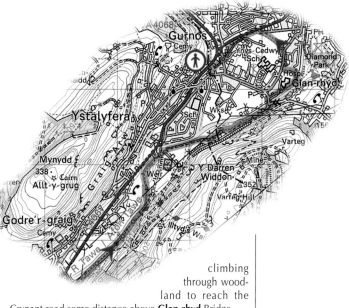

climbing
through wood-
land to reach the
Crynant road some distance above **Glan-rhyd** Bridge.

Drop down to cross the bridge and then take the first
right, eventually reaching a riverside path that skirts a
hospital and then, wholly unexpectedly, arrives at the distinctive remains of Ynyscedwyn ironworks, well worth a
gentle exploration. From the ironworks, cross the B4599
and follow a footpath just past The Grove care home to
discover another surprise – the dewatered Ynyscedwyn
branch canal, some 800m in length and, in parts, a heavily wooded deep trench. The footpath follows the south
bank of the former waterway.

Iron smelting at **Ynyscedwyn ironworks** dates back
to at least 1612, although industrial activity was at
its height in the early 19th century. In 1837, the hot
blast method of smelting with anthracite alone was
developed at Ynyscedwyn. By 1860, more than a
thousand men were employed at the ironworks,
operating seven furnaces, yet within 20 years it
was outdated and in decline. Later, the Welsh
Tinplate Company used the site until the furnaces

Ynyscedwyn ironworks

were finally abandoned in the 1940s. The surviving arches, almost reminiscent of a ruined abbey, occupy a surprisingly tranquil location close to a number of urban villages.

Turn left just before reaching the A4067, walking alongside the road before dropping down to follow the rather forlorn main line of the canal on its journey across a roundabout and through **Gurnos**. This leads to another impressive sight: a spectacular three-arched aqueduct, which carried the canal over the Afon Twrch. This is close to the site where the Gurnos corn mill was built in 1889 and where the primitive Palleg railway delivered coal and iron ore from workings in Cwm Twrch to Gurnos Wharf on the canal. ◄

Coal and iron ore descended an incline to the canal by gravity and teams of horses hauled the empty wagons back to the top.

From the aqueduct, a short path leads to the modern road bridge over the Twrch and from there to the little town of **Ystalyfera** and the end of the walk.

WALK 3
The Cwm Cregan Trail

Start/Finish	Glyncorrwg Ponds visitor centre (SS 872 984)
Distance	6 miles (10km)
Ascent	150m (490ft)
Time	2–3hrs
Map(s)	Explorer 166
Public transport	Buses 32 and 36 run frequently from Bridgend and Maesteg to Cymer, with an hourly shuttle service from Cymer to Glyncorrwg.

There is inspirational walking in the Afan Valley, which was devastated by the closures of its collieries in the 1970s but transformed by community-led green tourism. It boasts world-class mountain bike trails, Glyncorrwg Ponds (offering fishing, canoeing and wildlife watching) and some excellent walking routes. The Cwm Cregan Trail passes the so-called grottos at Abercregan and returns to Glyncorrwg along the line of a former mineral railway, with a diversion to the curious Refreshment Rooms at Cymer.

The walk starts from **Glyncorrwg** Ponds, part of a concerted effort to regenerate this relatively isolated area following the closure in 1970 of Glyncorrwg Colliery, which employed around a thousand miners in the 1920s. The region is now internationally renowned for mountain biking, with a series of trails snaking through the Forestry Commission's Afan Forest Park.

The Cwm Cregan Trail climbs steeply up the hillside opposite the last of the ponds, first disentangling itself

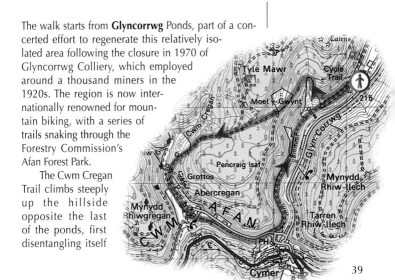

The ruins of Ty'n-y-pant Farm

from a cycle trail and then gaining height through larch plantations on a delightful path cushioned by pine needles to reach a viewpoint down the Corrwg Valley. A series of zigzags follows, reaching the ghostly, lichened ruins of Ty'n-y-pant Farm in a hollow on the edge of the forest. The trail then rises more gently, turning left on a broad path and crossing the shoulder of **Pencraig Isaf**, with increasingly impressive views across the rolling, wooded hills of Coed Morgannwg.

Cross the flat top of the hill, with occasional views to the left into the Corrwg Valley, before joining a forest road at a hairpin bend (take the right-hand road here) and following it as it drops down into **Cwm Cregan**. There is a sudden, startling view of the Ffynnon Oer windfarm. Descend on a track that starts stony but becomes grassy as it hugs a hillside bench and then reaches the valley floor near Troed y Rhiw, curving round to pass just to the north of the Abercregan grottos. ◄

In reality, the grottos are caverns created by quarrymen in search of stone slabs. The caverns are unstable and there have been roof falls, and they are now inaccessible.

The track leads directly to the village of **Abercregan**, a classic example of industrial growth and decline. It enjoyed a mining boom in the 19th century and endured

a long decline from the 1970s onwards. Much of the workers' housing has been demolished and while the valley is now pleasant and rural, the village is a shadow of its former self. Beyond the Little Chapel in Hopkins Terrace the route joins the Afan Valley cycleway, laid over the tracks of the South Wales Mineral Railway, a broad gauge railway that operated goods trains between Glyncorrwg, Tonmawr and the docks at Briton Ferry.

The cycleway heads east towards Cymer, passing a fine lattice girder viaduct that carried yet another railway over the River Afan. Turn right across a road bridge on reaching Cymer to find the Refreshment Rooms, a single storey stone building, which once served as the buffet and waiting room for Cymer Afan station on the Rhondda and Swansea Bay railway (now also reduced to a cycleway!). ▶

Cross the River Afan again to return to the tarmac path on the line of the mineral railway as it follows the attractively wooded valley of the River Corrwg back to Glyncorrwg Ponds, passing a curious brick memorial on the site of the former Nantewlaeth Colliery, the deepest

Abercregan and the Afan Valley

The Refresh, as it is known locally, is now a pub and restaurant and well used by locals, cyclists and walkers.

41

coal mine in the area. The ponds are attractively landscaped and well stocked with a variety of fish including
trout, carp, bream, tench and roach. The picturesque setting is ideal for gentle lakeside walking at the end of the
Cwm Cregan Trail, with plants including primrose, flag
iris and purple loosestrife, and provides opportunities
for birdwatching, with heron, sandpipers and pied flycatchers often glimpsed on the lake or in the valley-side
woodland.

WALK 4

The Taff Trail

Start	Cardiff Castle (ST 180 766)
Finish	Ynysangharad Park, Pontypridd (ST 074 902)
Distance	15 miles (24km)
Ascent	220m (720ft)
Time	6–8hrs
Map(s)	Explorer 151, 166
Public transport	There is a very frequent train service between Cardiff and Pontypridd.

The oldest of the long-distance trails in the South Wales valleys, the Taff
Trail runs from Cardiff to Brecon. This route traces the lower valleys section,
mainly using old tramroads and the towpath of the Glamorganshire Canal –
very attractive to look at in places, less easy to find in others. The riverside
parklands north of Cardiff city centre and the Gothic folly of Castell Coch
dominate the lower section of the trail, all on surfaced paths, while the
ancient bridge at Pontypridd is a worthy destination.

Walk towards the river from the main entrance to **Cardiff
Castle**, successively a Roman fort, medieval castle and
sumptuous Victorian mansion. Turn into Bute Park, the
southern element of a sublime network of parklands
stretching north from the city centre, and keep close to

the banks of the River Taff as the trail passes the remains of the Blackfriars Priory and a suspension bridge at Blackweir. This southern section of the trail is very busy with cyclists, joggers, dog-walkers and family strollers, as well as trail walkers, although the congestion eases once you've passed underneath Western Avenue.

The route hugs the eastern bank of the Taff, with the spire of Llandaff Cathedral, a religious site since the sixth century but ruinous after the Reformation and badly damaged by bombing in World War II, strikingly visible across the river. A tour through the suburb of **Llandaff North** leads to an under-publicised gem: the water pump at the former Melingriffith tinplate works, which is actually a water lift installed in the 1790s to lift water from the Melingriffith feeder to the Glamorganshire Canal. ▸

The next mile or so is equally

The device was neglected for years after the canal closed in 1942 but restored in 1980 and again in 2010.

Map continues on page 45

impressive, offering a choice between following the river past the listed farmhouse at Forest Farm or taking the towpath of the Glamorganshire Canal through a nature reserve and past an example of a Glamorganshire lock, one of very few to survive.

*The restored
Melingriffith water lift*

One of the more successful Welsh canals, the **Glamorganshire Canal** opened to traffic in February 1794. The first boat took 20 hours to travel the 24½ miles (39.5km) from Merthyr to Cardiff, negotiating 49 locks on the way. By 1830, seven-day working had been introduced and lighting installed to allow boats to move at night. Cargo peaked at 350,000 tonnes in 1839, but two years later the railway reached Merthyr and traffic seeped away.

The routes converge just south of the M4, where the track passes a weir, dives beneath the motorway and reaches an iron bridge. ◀

*The bridge originally
carried the
Melingriffith tramway
across the river.*

Detour left here for an impressive view of Castell Coch, but go back to take a narrow lane leading into **Tongwynlais**. Turn left along the main road, then right before the Lewis Arms to take the road leading to Castell Coch. Ignore two signposted paths on the left; instead take the main entrance drive to the castle, which rises quite steeply but has the sudden reward of an amazing prospect of the fairytale Gothic castle.

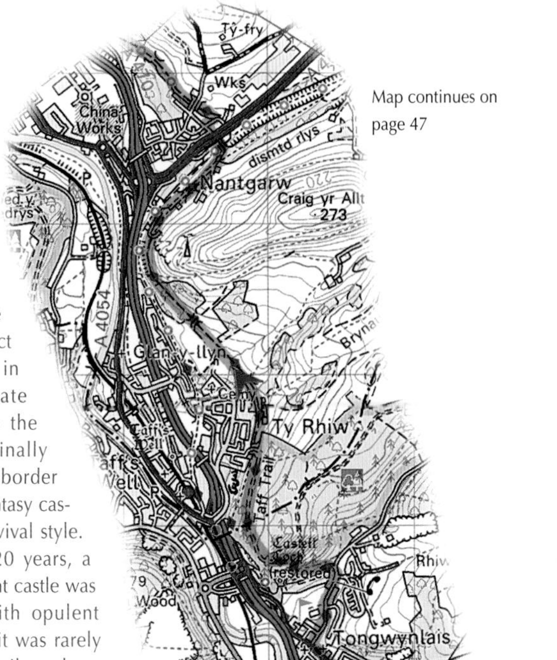

Map continues on page 47

Not satisfied with remodeling Cardiff Castle into a Victorian Gothic mansion, the Bute family commissioned the eccentric architect William Burges in 1871 to recreate **Castell Coch** – the red castle, originally a 13th-century border fortress – as a fantasy castle in Gothic Revival style. Over the next 20 years, a wildly extravagant castle was constructed, with opulent furnishings; yet it was rarely visited by the family and soon became little more than a folly.

Take the signposted track that climbs steadily north of the castle, turn left onto a broad track when the slope eases, and hug the eastern side of the Taff gorge, going gently downhill but still well above the valley floor. At the height of the industrial revolution, at a time when the canal was still functioning, no fewer than six railway lines ran through the narrow gorge. This is a particularly enjoyable section of the trail, with rapid progress possible through open birch woodland, which screens the industrial estates in the valley.

At Ty Rhiw, on the outskirts of **Taffs Well**, the trail passes a bridge over an abandoned length of the

45

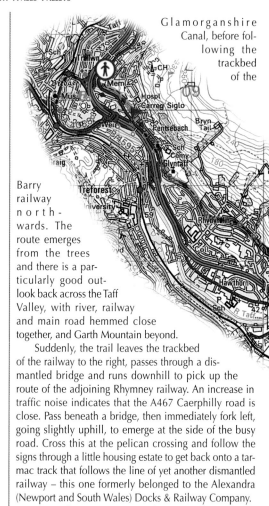

Glamorganshire Canal, before following the trackbed of the Barry railway northwards. The route emerges from the trees and there is a particularly good outlook back across the Taff Valley, with river, railway and main road hemmed close together, and Garth Mountain beyond.

Suddenly, the trail leaves the trackbed of the railway to the right, passes through a dismantled bridge and runs downhill to pick up the route of the adjoining Rhymney railway. An increase in traffic noise indicates that the A467 Caerphilly road is close. Pass beneath a bridge, then immediately fork left, going slightly uphill, to emerge at the side of the busy road. Cross this at the pelican crossing and follow the signs through a little housing estate to get back onto a tarmac track that follows the line of yet another dismantled railway – this one formerly belonged to the Alexandra (Newport and South Wales) Docks & Railway Company.

The trail now negotiates a long, straight and well-wooded cutting on a bench above the valley floor and the traffic noise quickly disappears. A bridge carries the Eglwysilan road over the trail at the site of Groeswen station, where the relict platforms are still visible. To the north of the old station, a deep rock cutting is followed by a section that has wide views across the Taff Valley.

The route becomes a little suburban as it enters **Rhydyfelin**, heading through a little park and then running between housing estates and a huge cemetery, which is an unlikely wildlife hotspot. Taff Trail signposts proliferate but also irritate – several in succession proclaim that the distance to Pontypridd is still 1½ miles (2.5km)! An unavoidable section of road walking follows, but it is worth persevering to see one final and highly unlikely manifestation of the Glamorganshire Canal. To discover this, just after passing a footbridge over the A470, follow the signs to Nightingale's Bush. Around 400m of the old canal remains, with a footpath alongside, which runs behind the Bunch of Grapes, an outstanding pub and restaurant. The highlight is the site of a two-chamber staircase lock. Once the path ends, pass under the dual carriageway to reach Ynysangharad Park and the centre of **Pontypridd**.

WALK 5

Along the Monmouthshire and Brecon Canal

Start	Pontymoel marina (SO 292 001)
Finish	Llanfoist Wharf (SO 285 130)
Distance	11 miles (18km)
Ascent	Negligible
Time	4–5hrs
Map(s)	Explorer 152, Outdoor Leisure 13
Public transport	Buses X3 and X33 connect Cardiff and Newport hourly with both Pontymoel and Abergavenny, 1 mile (1.5km) north-east of Llanfoist.

Fully opened by 1812, the canal provided the market towns of Brecon and Abergavenny, and more importantly the industrial enterprises in Blaenavon and Pontypool, with a route to market via Newport docks. Much of the canal has been restored and from Pontymoel northwards it runs through increasingly attractive countryside, contouring around the hillsides on the west side of the Usk Valley and passing the once-important wharves at Goytre and Llanfoist.

Start by finding Pontymoel marina. It is tucked below a dual carriageway heading for Pontypool but is a haven of tranquility, with a tiny canal basin, a fine stone bridge

A hire boat on the canal near Mamhilad

and Junction Cottage, built in 1814 as a toll house. Tolls were collected from traffic using the two canals that merged here – the Monmouthshire, which ascended a flight of 11 locks to Pontnewynydd (the canal was drained and the bed reused for a railway in 1854) and the Brecknock and Abergavenny, a contour canal, which rises just 18m (60ft) in the course of its 33-mile (53km) journey. Boats are available to hire for the day at Pontymoel, and there is a café located next to the marina.

The canal crosses the Afon Lwyd on a high aqueduct and heads north-east, passing above the tiny church at **Llanfihangel Pontymoel**

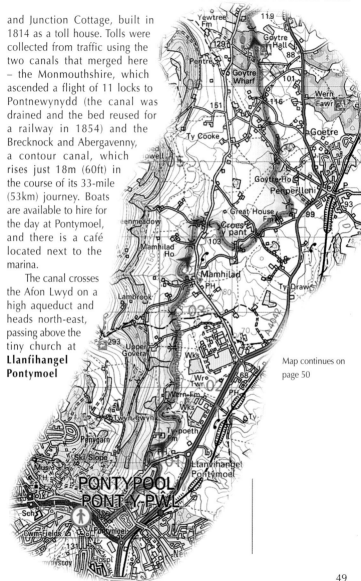

Map continues on
page 50

49

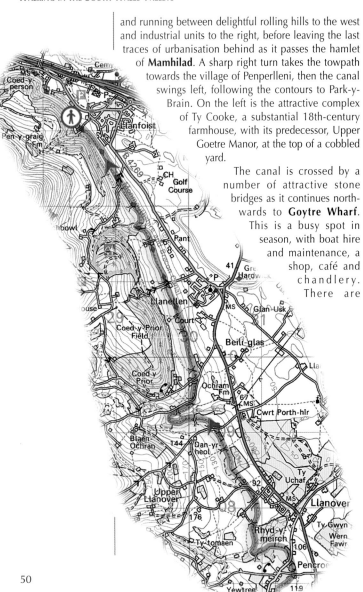

and running between delightful rolling hills to the west and industrial units to the right, before leaving the last traces of urbanisation behind as it passes the hamlet of **Mamhilad**. A sharp right turn takes the towpath towards the village of Penperlleni, then the canal swings left, following the contours to Park-y-Brain. On the left is the attractive complex of Ty Cooke, a substantial 18th-century farmhouse, with its predecessor, Upper Goetre Manor, at the top of a cobbled yard.

The canal is crossed by a number of attractive stone bridges as it continues northwards to **Goytre Wharf**. This is a busy spot in season, with boat hire and maintenance, a shop, café and chandlery. There are

Goytre Wharf

well-preserved historic remains, including substantial lime kilns, which hint at a prosperous industrial past. Beyond Ty Porth and another tight right-hand bend, the canal skirts **Llanover**, an estate village presided over in the 1840s by the staunch Methodist and strict teetotaller Lady Llanover, who turned the village into an oasis of Welshness and banned alcohol – the nearest pub is the excellent Goose and Cuckoo, high on the mountainside, just beyond the boundaries of the estate.

North of Llanover, the towpath follows the canal under Ty-coch Bridge and then around the Ochram Turn, a picturesque detour around the valley of the Ochram Brook, which is crossed on a solid aqueduct. The disused Ochram mill lies below, with the replanted ancient woodland of Coed y Prior ahead to the left, beyond Poplar Bridge on another sharp bend that narrowboats can find challenging. Below the wood, which was once in the possession of Abergavenny Priory, lies Ty Aur (the 'house of gold') – so-called because an aureus, or gold coin, of Claudius dated to AD51 was found here, although the nature of the Roman presence in this spot is uncertain.

A long straight length of canal then follows, with the distinctive little mountain of Skirrid Fawr forming a

Llanfoist Wharf

Castell Prydydd is a solid farmhouse dating from the 16th century but substantially rebuilt over the years. Legend has it that the house was exchanged for a mountain in the mid-19th century.

Trams laden with pig iron, coal and limestone were lowered to the wharf, their weight being used to raise trams laden with farm produce and beer from the Llanfoist Brewery up to the tramroad.

scenic backdrop beyond the village of **Llanellen** to the right (the curious offset spire of the village church can just be glimpsed) and the wooded slopes of the Blorenge rising up to the left. An accommodation bridge carries local traffic from Bridge Farm over the canal, with another tight double bend as the canal hugs the valley side around the little stream coming down from Middle Ninfa. Castell Prydydd (the 'poet's castle') is, however, tantalisingly out of sight. ◄

Finally, beyond Canal Cottage and another attractive stone-built bridge, the towpath reaches **Llanfoist** Wharf, in a beautiful wooded setting, and with fascinating evidence of a busy industrial past. A narrow tunnel carries the former parish road under the canal. A warehouse was formerly used to store iron from Garnddyrys forge near Blaenavon, and a wharfinger's house incorporates the former wheel house at the foot of the three-stage incline, which was used to transfer products from tramroads originating in Blaenavon ironworks to the canal. ◄

A boat hire business uses the wharf and its boat houses as the base for trips along one of the most scenic canals in the country.

WALK 6
The Usk Valley Walk

Start	Twyn Square, Usk (SO 377 009)
Finish	Llanellen Bridge (SO 305 110)
Distance	12 miles (19km)
Ascent	150m (490ft)
Time	5–7hrs
Map(s)	Explorer 152, Outdoor Leisure 13
Public transport	Usk has bus connections to Newport (service 60) approximately every hour. Abergavenny, a five-minute bus journey (X3 and X33) from Llanellen, has frequent trains to Newport.

This stretch of the Usk Valley Walk offers easy walking. It often runs close to the river, with stunning views upstream to the mountains in places, but sometimes climbs onto the valley sides. The main attraction, though, is the wealth of historic sites on or close to the walk, including the attractive market town of Usk, the marvellous church at Bettws Newydd, the Iron Age hillfort (carpeted with bluebells in spring) at Coed y Bwnydd, and the National Trust's Clytha Castle.

From Twyn Square, overlooked by Usk Castle, walk down Bridge Street, passing the Three Salmons Hotel, with its stabling and ostler's bell. Cross the river at the bridge and take the riverside footpath, going through the little park on The Island and then under the rusty iron girders of a long-abandoned railway bridge. The footpath is very well-defined, with the river on the right and the first of several enormous fields, usually cropped with maize, to the left. Swing away from the river through woodland and cross and re-cross a tributary stream – heron and grey partridge can be seen here and Usk College is on the left.

Turn left along a narrow lane, and then right (it is well signposted, as is generally the case with this walk) to skirt around another field of maize, with oak woodland on the river cliff to the right. A break in the woodland

Map continues on
page 55

In the medieval period, Estavarney was a grange farm of Tintern Abbey.

reveals a field of solar panels in front of Llancayo Farm, before the route becomes a track, heading down to the big rambling farm estate at **Estavarney**. ◀

The harvest at Estavarney

Take the lane north-west, turn right onto a way-marked path, and keep to the right initially to locate a path heading for a stile in the far corner of the field. When confronted by a green hill, contour round this to the right to a stile, which gives access to woodland. Follow a pleasant track down to the River Usk.

There might be a brief moment of uncertainty caused by a half-hidden signpost, but go right past an old pumping station to locate a path

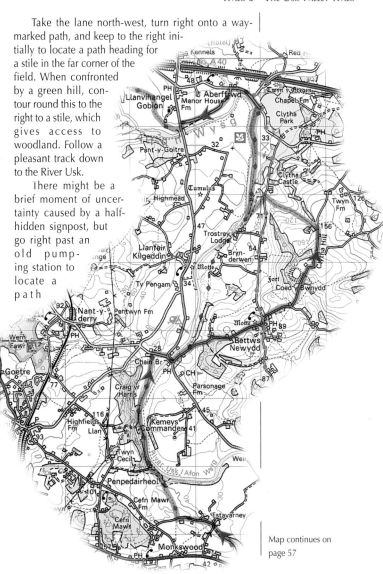

Map continues on page 57

55

that runs alongside the river. Use a green track to reach a country lane at Glan-usk. Turn right here to reach the bold, green Chain Bridge, which spans the Usk. ◀

Chain Bridge was built by Brown Lenox of Pontypridd in 1829, replacing an earlier solid oak bridge. Although it was replaced in 1906, the name lingers. Coracle fishing was practised here as recently as the 1920s.

A lane heads uphill to **Bettws Newydd**; the official route leaves this to the left after 300m for an easy but uneventful ramble, but it is much more rewarding to follow the lane uphill all the way to Bettws Newydd. It has a small delightful church, its centrepiece a superb intact medieval rood screen. An even narrower lane then leads uphill to the fort and nature reserve at Coed y Bwnydd.

The Iron Age hillfort at **Coed y Bwnydd**, with substantial ramparts to the east, defended a massive enclosure, and was reused later – medieval longhouses were discovered during excavations. The ramparts are covered in bluebells in spring, and its nature reserve is well known for its display of orchids.

Bluebells on the ramparts at Coed y Bwnydd

To regain the riverside walk, continue up the lane to Clytha Hill, an attractive viewpoint, and take the bridleway and then a path to drop down to Trostrey Lodge, a

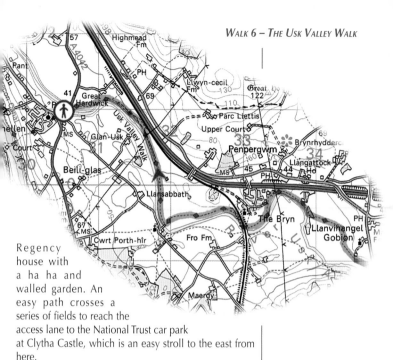

Regency
house with
a ha ha and
walled garden. An
easy path crosses a
series of fields to reach the
access lane to the National Trust car park
at Clytha Castle, which is an easy stroll to the east from
here.

> **Clytha Castle** is a castellated folly built by a griev-
> ing squire 'to relieve a mind afflicted by the loss of
> a most excellent wife'. It was intended to be seen
> against the sky from the much older Clytha House
> below, and to be used for grand picnics or as a
> retreat.

There is further easy riverside walking, which ends
after Weaver's Pool when the river swings left and the
path reaches a fairly busy road. Use the wide grass verge
to the left here, then turn left by the disused Aberffrwd
corn mill into a lane heading for **Pant-y-Goitre Bridge**. A
worthwhile diversion here of less than a mile (1km) leads
to the remarkable church at Llanfair Kilgeddin. Its inter-
nal walls are decorated in rich sgraffito, an ancient Italian
process applied by Heywood Sumner in the 1880s. ▶

The church is owned
by the Friends of
Friendless Churches
and is accessible via
a local keyholder.

Otherwise, take the path just before the bridge, crossing fields (a useful white signpost gives the direction across the second of these) and swinging left alongside an abandoned meander loop of the Usk, whose course is clear from the ponds dotting the Explorer map. The path rejoins the river bank, where there are excellent views upstream to the Blorenge and the Sugar Loaf, and **Llangatwg Dyffryn Wysg** church to the right.

Go under a railway viaduct and cross two more fields to reach two oddities in quick succession. First is a decrepit redbrick pillbox, which sits unexpectedly in the corner of a field, a relic of World War II now used only as a shelter for animals. Second is a private suspension bridge, which gives access across the river for the privileged few to **Llanover** church, with its 14th-century tower.

Stick close to the river past a rounded mound, which is all that hints at the presence of Castle Arnold, destroyed in the late 12th century. There is a stiff climb up wooden steps just south of the solid farmhouse at Great Hardwick, and one final riverside section before the three-arched **Llanellen** Bridge, built in 1821 by John Upton of Gloucester, appears to the right of the little village, which has a shop, tearoom and bus connections.

2 THE WESTERN RIDGES

Ffaldau and the Garw Valley (Walk 7)

WALK 7
Mynydd Garn-Fach and the upper Lliw Valley

Start/Finish	Felindre (SN 636 027)
Distance	7½ miles (12km)
Ascent	260m (855ft)
Time	3–4hrs
Map(s)	Explorer 165
Public transport	Service 142 provides a bus every two hours between Swansea and Felindre.

This is a superb walk in the unexpectedly varied countryside of upland Gower, only a few miles from Swansea yet hidden away in rolling countryside. The route climbs up to the windswept common land of Mynydd Garn-Fach and Mynydd y Gwair before heading back alongside the two picturesque Lliw reservoirs. Both provide good spots for birdwatching and the lower one is often busy with anglers.

From the main road through **Felindre**, take the Ammanford road and then turn immediately right into Heol Myddfai, passing the Shepherds Arms and the village school. Ignore the track on the left just beyond the school. It leads to Felindre Big Fish Water, a fishing lake on the site of the Blaen Nant Ddu reservoir, which was dismantled in the 1970s, although the fine stonework of the draw off tunnel can still be seen. Instead, take a track on the right at a signpost groaning with the weight of signs for the Gower Way, Swansea Walks and the reservoirs, heading for Lletty Thomas Farm. After another 100m, a path on the right heads diagonally across a field to reach a splendid, level green path on a bench above the valley. Go through several kissing gates; the view ahead is increasingly dominated by the earthen dam of the Lower Lliw reservoir.

The **Lliw Valley reservoirs** were built to supply water to the rapidly growing population of Swansea and its surrounding villages. The lower Lliw reservoir was completed in 1862 at a cost of £160,000.

Growing demand led to the construction of the upper reservoir some 30 years later, while the lower reservoir was reconstructed in the 1970s, with a new rock-filled dam, a new spillway and a recon-structed pumping station. There is a car park and outdated toilet block by the lower dam.

Keep ahead on a delightful track following the west bank of the reservoir, which is home to a variety of water birds and always offers the chance of seeing buzzards and red kites circling overhead. The reservoir tapers dramatically in its upper reaches, but the narrow path con-tinues ahead, eventually crossing the river on a wooden footbridge. Climb the steps opposite to reach the tarmac road, which provides access to the upper reservoir.

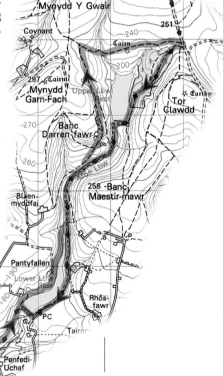

Keep to the road over a cattle grid and past a quarry. Immediately after a river bridge next to a stone Gower Way marker (number 44), scramble up to the left to reach a path climb-ing alongside telegraph poles onto Banc Darren Fawr and around the shoulder of **Mynydd Garn-Fach**. The views open out dramatically, with the rounded hill of Tor Clawdd seen across the valley and the outline of Torclawdd bungalow just to its left.

Looking across the lower Lliw reservoir

Torclawdd bungalow was built in 1934 by the eccentric scientist Harry Grindell Mathews, who worked here behind a high and electrified barbed wire fence. Mathews invented radio telephony, worked on submarine detection and developed the electric gun, which could immobilise combustion engines and exterminate vermin, and which gave him the sobriquet 'Death Ray' Matthews.

The path ascends the open common land on the eastern flanks of Mynydd Garn-Fach, passing close to the remains of two mines. There are superb views eastwards over the deep valley containing the upper reservoir and towards the summit of Tor Clawdd, its upper slopes curiously pitted by adits associated with coal mining. Turn right at a lonely crossroads onto a wider track, now heading east and dipping down to cross the infant Afon Lliw, before traversing **Mynydd y Gwair**, an unremarkable stretch of moorland now well known for the battle to halt plans for a windfarm on its slopes. ◄

The proposal for 19 turbines up to 127m (417ft) high was said to be designed carefully to blend with the local environment while providing sustainable clean energy, but has proved controversial and involved protracted planning inquiries and appeals.

The track peters out on the level, damp moorland but the way ahead is obvious, contouring above the upper

The Upper Lliw reservoir and Tor Clawdd

reservoir and the prominent Brynllefrith plantation, before reaching the lonely mountain road between Swansea and Ammanford. Turn right here and then quickly right again on a track that heads over a stile straight into the conifer woodland. Away to the left are the somewhat battered remains of the 10th-century Tor Clawdd dyke, with its long linear causeway, which controlled travellers through upland Gower.

A stony track leads through the sparse larch, Sitka spruce and Scots pine of Brynllefrith plantation. Follow the frequent waymarks to find a path that leads out of the plantation and alongside the upper reservoir, now on a narrow green track, which leads to a house right by the dam. The easiest route back to Felindre lies along the tarmac lane, with the Afon Lliw and then the lower reservoir on the right, although it is just as easy to cross the stream and return by the outward route alongside the west bank of the lower reservoir. In either case, the final leg retraces the initial part of the route below Lletty Thomas and down Heol Myddfai to the centre of Felindre.

WALK 8

The Gnoll, Melincourt Falls and the Neath Canal

Start/Finish	Neath Castle (SS 753 978)
Distance	12 miles (19km)
Ascent	330m (1080ft)
Time	4–6hrs
Map(s)	Explorer 165 (small section of route on Explorer 166)
Public transport	Neath has a frequent train service from Swansea and Cardiff.

A relatively short ridge walk and an easy return along the Neath Canal (opened in 1795) make for an excellent expedition, but it is not to be taken lightly! The route starts at Neath Castle and takes in the attractive Gnoll Estate Country Park, the tree-fringed Mosshouse reservoir and the huge Roman marching camp at Blaen-cwmbach. But the undoubted highlight is the superb Melincourt Falls, plunging 25m (80ft) over a rocky ledge.

From the centre of **Neath**, follow Alfred Street past the restored Victoria Gardens. Veer left and take Gnoll Gardens, going through two gates to enter the Gnoll Estate, the former pleasure grounds of the Mackworth family. Laid out in the 1740s, they include land-scaped gardens, a grotto, an ice house and the Gnoll Cascades. Keep to the left of two lakes, go past a café and head up into Mosshouse Wood, eventually reaching a straight track running along-

side an artificial watercourse. Pass a folly, turn left and climb steps to reach a car park and a country lane. Turn right along the lane to reach the picturesque Mosshouse reservoir.

Keep on the lane as it rises past the reservoir, with the romantic ruins of the **Ivy Tower** on the left. ▶

The slope eases and there is an excellent prospect across the valley, taking in Swansea Bay and the long whaleback of Hirfynydd, its summit ridge traversed by the Sarn Helen Roman road.

Go straight ahead on a rough track when the tarmac ends. Pelenna Forest is ahead and the village of Tonmawr is down to the right. After 200m, the low western rampart of the Roman marching camp at Blaen-cwmbach can be seen to the left.

Built in the 18th century as a banqueting house and viewing tower, the battlemented Ivy Tower was used as a gamekeeper's house until 1910, when it was destroyed by fire.

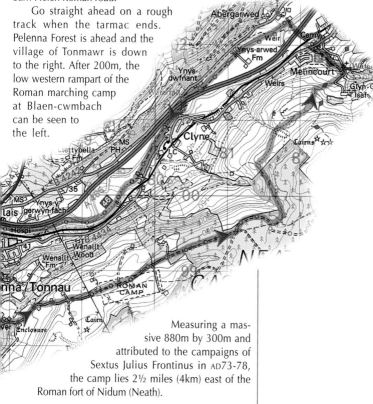

Measuring a massive 880m by 300m and attributed to the campaigns of Sextus Julius Frontinus in AD73-78, the camp lies 2½ miles (4km) east of the Roman fort of Nidum (Neath).

The route continues through two gates and past the remains of a round barrow into Pelenna Forest, taking a broad track through a surprisingly open plantation. At a junction of forest roads, the course of the old bridleway is obstructed by the trees; instead, keep to the left, curving round the edge of the forest and then taking another left turn, going downhill on a forest road around a sharp left-hand bend.

As the track bends right, keep straight on along a green lane, somewhat overgrown, which gradually loses height and reaches a gate at the edge of the forest. Go through the gate and keep to the right, contouring below the forest to reach an obvious track that crosses the Nant Dyfnant and runs below the ridge of Carn Caca, with its cairn circles and hut platforms. The upper Neath Valley and the town of Resolven are prominent to the left.

The track meets St Illtyd's Walk west of Glyn Gwilym Isaf. Turn left here, zigzagging down to meet a tarmac lane, and follow this as far as a gate on the left. Go through the gate on a path that leads along the top of the deep, wooded Melincourt gorge. The waterfall on the right is unseen but very loud. The path doubles back to reach the base of the waterfall, which crashes over a band of resistant Pennant Sandstone into a plunge pool 25m (82ft) below. ◀

Melincourt waterfall has been attracting visitors for some time – Turner painted here in 1795 – and is the centrepiece of a noted nature reserve, with woodpeckers, jays, dippers and wagtails.

Take the path along the gorge, often high above the stream, as far as the road through the village of **Melincourt**. Turn right here, then quickly left across a mineral railway and onto a path that dives under the A465 along with a rushing stream, and then over a footbridge that crosses the River Neath. Immediately turn left along an unsignposted track that passes a weir and, when the river peels away to the left, runs alongside the wildly overgrown bed of the Neath Canal – first evidenced by a bridge almost lost in the undergrowth and then by the dilapidated remains of the Abergarwed lock.

For a few hundred metres, the canal is heavily reduced in width by rushes, but from just north of the restored bridge serving Ynys-arwed Farm it has been painstakingly cleared, although the banks all the way to Neath are intermittently infested by Himalayan balsam.

Melincourt waterfall

The canal approaches the A465 and then dives left beneath it, emerging by the river, which is crossed on the impressively restored Ynysbwllog Aqueduct. ▶

The towpath can now be followed all the way to Neath, passing the double locks at **Clyne**, the Machin lock and, most picturesque of all, the junction with the Tennant Canal at **Aberdulais**. The towpath crosses the canal on a delightful angled stone bridge, runs alongside the Tennant basin and then heads under a railway bridge and across a road. Canal and river now run very close together at times, with the towpath running along a narrow strip of land between them. The restored Ty'n-yr-heol lock is followed by the ancient St Illtyd's Church, right on the canal bank in Llantwit-juxta-Neath. ▶

By now the suburbs of Neath are encroaching and, just beyond a road bridge, the canal widens into a basin. There is often a pleasure boat moored here – the Neath & Tennant Canals Trust runs trips on Saturdays in the summer, and more frequently in the summer holidays. Behind the Quaker meeting house, the gaunt remains of Neath Castle, which retains a magnificent 14th-century gatehouse, mark the end of the walk.

The central span of the aqueduct collapsed in the 1970s, but recent restoration has seen the installation of a 32m plate girder aqueduct, possibly the longest single-span aqueduct in Britain.

Built on the site of the sixth-century cell established by St Illtyd, the Norman church contains an unusual double-decker pulpit.

67

WALK 9

The Coed Morgannwg Way

Start	Margam Park (SS 802 863)
Finish	Dare Valley Country Park (SN 984 026)
Distance	27½ miles (44km)
Public transport	Buses X1 and 224 provide at least an hourly service to Margam from Port Talbot and Swansea, and less frequent service from Bridgend. Buses 32 and 36 run frequently from Bridgend and Maesteg to Cymer, a half-mile (0.8km) stroll (or infrequent morning bus ride) along the Afan Valley from Abercregan. Aberdare has half-hourly train and bus services to Cardiff.
Accommodation	If you wish to split the route with an overnight stop, accommodation options are very limited. Ty Dor in Abercregan (Tel 07805 423231) is aimed at self-catering but offers one-night lettings which may appeal to groups of walkers. Cymer has one bed and breakfast option (Bryn Teg House, Tel 01639 851820); an alternative is Queens Guesthouse in Glyncorrwg (Tel 01639 850487).

Well known as the most demanding of the long-distance paths in the valleys, but chronically under-signposted now that Forestry Commission Wales gives priority to short circular walks, the Coed Morgannwg Way is best tackled in (at least!) two stages.

The first stage runs from Margam Park, using ancient trackways as it passes prehistoric earthworks on its way to Afan Argoed and Cwm Cregan.

The second stage crosses remote, forested moorland to the summit of Craig y Llyn, before descending steadily to the Dare Valley Country Park near Aberdare. (A rather uninteresting extension carries on to Merthyr Tydfil but is not described here.)

The Coed Morgannwg Way above the Afan Valley

STAGE 1

Coed Morgannwg Way West

Start	Margam Park (SS 802 863)
Finish	Abercregan (SS 848 966)
Distance	14½ miles (23km)
Ascent	775m (2540ft)
Time	6–9hrs
Map(s)	Explorer 166 (two small sections of the route are on Explorer 165)

The first section of the Coed Morgannwg Way runs from the historic landscape of Margam Park, past prehistoric earthworks to the main ridge. It reuses ancient trackways as it threads its way through the forest to Afan Argoed, then passes a ruined Methodist chapel and a farm fossilised in the plantations, before descending into Cwm Cregan.

From the ruins of Margam Abbey and the adjacent Margam Stones Museum, with its collection of rare early Christian inscribed stones and Celtic crosses (including the sixth-century Bodvoc stone – see below), the Way runs along the west bank of a fishpond well-stocked with wildfowl. It then rounds Mynydd y Castell, crowned by an Iron Age promontory fort that was reused in the early medieval period. There are excellent views over **Margam Park**, now a country park that includes a mansion and an impressive 18th-century orangery. The Glamorgan Ridgeway heads east from here, but the Coed Morgannwg Way climbs the valley of Cwm Philip, with every chance of glimpsing fallow deer, before climbing onto the high plateau of Mynydd Margam, with its wealth of prehistoric features.

Map continues on page 72

The remote uplands behind the coastal plain at Margam and Port Talbot have seen a wide variety of human intervention, each contributing to the current richly diversified landscape of **Coed Morgannwg**. Prehistoric man has left traces of primitive settlement, burial cairns and ancient trackways; at its height, the Cistercian monastery of Margam ran the area as an upland sheepwalk controlled by grange farms. In the 20th century, man saw the potential for large-scale forestry, much of which has now matured and been felled, and later for recreation, including mountain biking. The Pen y Cymoedd windfarm may dramatically change the landscape again in the near future.

The route passes the well-defined double-banked Iron Age enclosure of Caer Blaen-y-Cwm at the head of Cwm Kenfig. Turn left here onto Heol y Moch, one of several ancient trackways crossing these uplands, before passing to the left of **Twmpath Diwlith** (a prominent Bronze Age round barrow, which when excavated revealed a cist containing fragmentary bones and covered by turf). ▶

The substantial earthworks of Y Bwlwarcau, a multi-phase hillfort with a pentagonal enclosure superimposed on earlier concentric defences, lie a little lower down the slope to the east. There is a real sense of walking through history here, in a landscape that has been continuously occupied for thousands of years.

The route lies north to Carreg Bica, then west through the forest, skirting Maesteg golf course and dropping down to the old mining settlement of **Bryn**. Take a gravel track across old colliery workings; turn right before a gate and head east through clearfell and around a narrow valley to reach a crossroads of forest tracks. Turn left here, uphill, following white arrows painted on rocks in the absence of formal waymarks. Ignore a strange diversion to the east; instead keep straight on, cresting a rise by a pool with rushes and water lilies, and walk towards a

Nearby is a replica of the sixth-century Bodvoc stone, an early inscribed boundary marker.

Map continues on
page 75

huge sheepwalk. Take the forest road on the left and stay
on this as it runs between conifer plantations and then
crosses a large area of clearfell, zigzagging down into

Cwm Argoed, with a pleasant tree-fringed stream to the left.

The route reaches the main road just to the west of the **Afan Argoed** Country Park visitor centre. Go straight under the road and across an impressive footbridge over the River Afan. Go left to meet and follow an abandoned railway down the valley, before backtracking higher up the slope, passing the grassy banks of a medieval house platform to reach the ruins of the medieval Gyfylchi chapel of ease, once an important centre for local Methodists. ▶

The route now lies high above the Afan Valley. Go straight on when a forest road peels off to the right and take a green path running between gorse, heather, bilberries and brambles on its way to a bench with a bird's-eye view down the valley. A section on a forest road follows; at a complex junction turn right, passing the well-preserved ruins of a 17th-century longhouse at Nant-y-Bar. ▶

The forest road runs below the craggy slopes of Mynydd Rhiwgregan to reach the side valley of Cwm Cregan. The road ends abruptly here, metamorphosing

Gyfylchi also has a welcoming café, bike hire and an exceptional outlook northwards, over Pelenna Forest. Nant y bar Farm was extended in 1810 and became more prosperous when coal was discovered on the farm in the mid-19th century.

Pelenna Forest from Gyfylchi

The ruins of Nant-y-bar Farm

into a green path, which drops through woodland to a dilapidated stile. Turn right, crossing the stream and angling up on a green path to reach a track leading into the village of Abercregan.

STAGE 2
Coed Morgannwg Way East

Start	Abercregan (SS 848 966)
Finish	Dare Valley Country Park (SN 984 026)
Distance	13 miles (21km)
Ascent	540m (1770ft)
Time	6–8hrs
Map(s)	Explorer 166

The second half of the Coed Morgannwg Way explores moorland and woodland as remote as anything in South Wales. It follows the edge of the escarpment above the Vale of Neath as far as Craig y Llyn, the highest point in the region, and then heads across open moorland to the unexpectedly scenic Dare Valley, above Aberdare.

Take the lane heading north-west up Cwm Cregan, then drop down on a green path to cross the Nant Cregan. Continue on a rough track, which climbs alongside an attractive mountain stream, aiming for Cefnmawr and the high plateau. Initially, there are wind turbines to the left, followed by stunning views of the Black Mountain and Fforest Fawr as the Way, following a broad forest track, passes just to the north of the Bronze Age cairn and boundary marker at Carn Caglau.

Map continues on page 76

The Coed Morgannwg Way is now following another ancient trackway, the crucially important ridgeway of Cefn Ffordd, which keeps to the high ground as it follows the ridge north-east-wards towards the head of the Rhondda Valleys. There is one moment of uncertainty, at a junction of forest roads half a mile (0.8km) north-east of Carn Caglau. Cefn Ffordd goes straight on, but its route is poorly signposted and obscured by vegetation as it dips

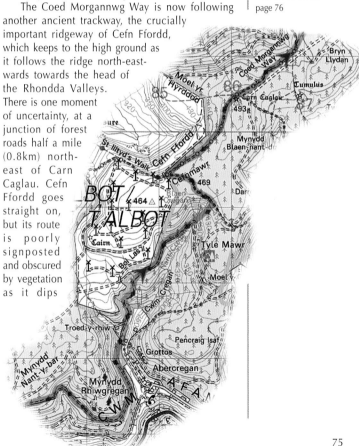

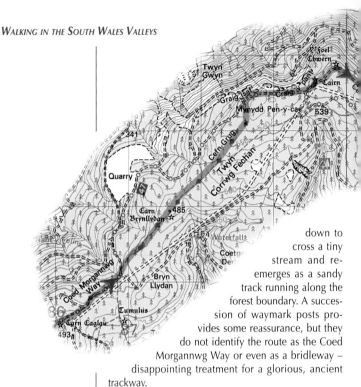

down to cross a tiny stream and re-emerges as a sandy track running along the forest boundary. A succession of waymark posts provides some reassurance, but they do not identify the route as the Coed Morgannwg Way or even as a bridleway – disappointing treatment for a glorious, ancient trackway.

Keep on past yet another burial mound at Carn Brynllydan, drop down to Bwlch Ffos and climb again along Cefn Grug, a good vantage point for sightings of brown hares and, high in the forest, breeding crossbills. Buzzards and, increasingly, red kites soar above as the path reaches Mynydd Pen-y-cae and Craig y pant. The Way now teeters on a forest road above the steep scarp slope on the southern side of the Neath Valley. A relict Coed Morgannwg Way signpost points the way left towards the Dare Valley, now on a stony track through woodland above Y Foel Chwern.

Beyond the viewpoint, high above Llyn Fach, the route passes close to the Carn Fach burial mound and the trig point marking the summit of **Craig y Llyn**, at 600m (1968ft) the highest point in Wales, south of the Brecon

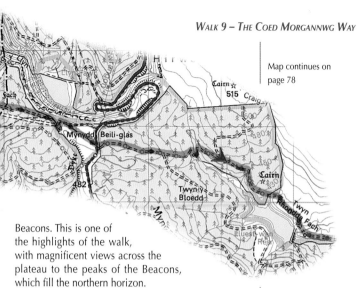

Map continues on
page 78

Beacons. This is one of
the highlights of the walk,
with magnificent views across the
plateau to the peaks of the Beacons,
which fill the northern horizon.

Go straight across a forest road, where passage along the Cefn Ffordd ridgeway was interrupted by another cross dyke, Ffos Toncenglau, which was thrown up in the eighth or ninth century and runs for three-quarters of a mile (1.2km) across the ridge. At a stile 200m further on, follow the path to the left, rounding the head of a minor valley and continuing alongside a fence. Down to the left is the big corrie lake of Llyn Fawr, though this is better seen from the A4061, which somewhat surprisingly appears straight ahead. ▸

Llyn Fawr hosts rich
moorland wildlife,
including ring ouzel,
linnet and whinchat,
and a range of
montane and alpine
plants on the steep
sandstone cliff face.

*Llyn Fawr from
Mynydd Beili-glas*

77

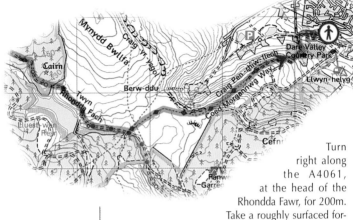

Turn right along the A4061, at the head of the Rhondda Fawr, for 200m. Take a roughly surfaced forest road along the ridge of **Mynydd Beili-glas**, heading east and zigzagging down to cross a stream near the medieval pound at Ffald Lluest-boeth and then crossing moorland to reach Lluest-wen reservoir. Below the reservoir the route keeps close to the infant Rhondda Fach River as far as the early 19th-century single-arched bridge at Pont Lluest-wen. Climb half-left and cross the open

The Dare Valley from Pen-rhiw-llech

moorland on a distinct path to reach a vantage point above the U-shaped Dare Valley, with the cliffs of Craig-yr-Ysgol and Tarren y Bwllfa at its head. This is a really attractive finale to the walk, which descends Craig Pen-rhiw-llech on a superb green path and then crosses moor-land above the lakes of the **Dare Valley Country Park** to reach the end of an epic journey at the visitor centre, complete with café and hotel.

WALK 10
Between the Llynfi and Garw

Start	Navigation Hotel, Caerau (ST 856 942)
Finish	Pont Rhyd-y-cyff (ST 869 889)
Distance	9½ miles (15km)
Ascent	560m (1840ft)
Time	4–6hrs
Map(s)	Explorer 166
Public transport	Trains run every hour between Cardiff, Bridgend and Maesteg, with a connecting bus service to Caerau. Pont Rhyd-y-cyff is close to Garth station on the same railway line.

This is a leisurely exploration of two of the more unchanged valleys, and of the high land between them. There is still evidence of the area's coal mining past, with the remains of old mines, levels, tips and railway viaducts, but much has been done to soften the impact, with green oases such as the Darren Valley south-east of Maesteg and increasingly sympathetic afforestation in the uplands. Wide-ranging views take in the Gower Peninsula, Exmoor and the Quantocks.

From the Navigation Hotel in the centre of the old min-ing village of **Caerau**, the route zigzags uphill through suburban terraces for a short distance. Take Library Road, Greenfield Terrace and Pleasant View, and then continue on a narrow lane with Caerau Primary School to the right. Just before the lane crosses a stream, turn left on an

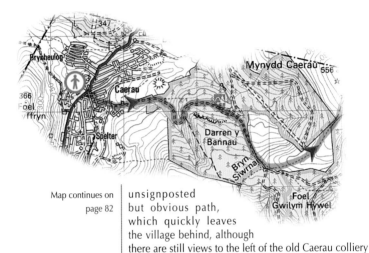

Map continues on page 82

Opened in 1890, Caerau colliery had three shafts and at its height employed 2400 miners. It closed in 1977.

unsignposted but obvious path, which quickly leaves the village behind, although there are still views to the left of the old Caerau colliery site. ◄

The path, already in delightfully sylvan surroundings, climbs steadily alongside the Nant Gwyn Bach (the 'small white stream') and then joins a forest road – it is much easier to follow this than the footpath alternative shown on the map. The road passes disused levels and then winds right and left through recent clearfell, before passing below the cliffs of **Darren y Bannau**. Once the site of a farmstead (a ruined sheepfold can still be seen) and then the scene of mining activity, this area is now a tranquil oasis, which is home to bullfinches, siskins and even flocks of the often elusive crossbill.

Take the right-hand forest road, slightly uphill, at the eastern end of Darren y Bannau, and keep ahead when this turns sharp right. Open fields will appear on the left as the track climbs steadily to reach **Bryn Siwrnai**, where displaying goshawks can often be seen in early spring. Just beyond a copse on the left, take the path heading over a stile and across a huge upland sheep pasture. After a gate, divert slightly left, passing low tumuli on the way to the lonely summit of Llyndwr Fawr.

Caerau and the Afan Valley from Llyndwr Fawr

The summit plateau of **Llyndwr Fawr**, while thronged with skylarks in spring and summer, is flat and largely featureless, but at 555m (1820ft) it offers a sensational view, taking in the Bristol Channel, Exmoor, Swansea Bay and the Gower Peninsula, and the Brecon Beacons.

Head north-east, passing above the rocks of Craig Walter, to reach another complex junction of paths at the narrow col of Bwlchgarw. Just before the junction, the path negotiates a cross dyke, which was built in the eighth or ninth century to impede movement along the ridge.

Turn right just beyond the col to descend on a rocky, eroded bridleway, now heading south and negotiating a curious little cattle grid to enter coniferous woodland. The path is light and airy and there are two forest roads to be negotiated (turn right then left on each occasion) on the way down to **Blaengarw** at the head of the Garw Valley.

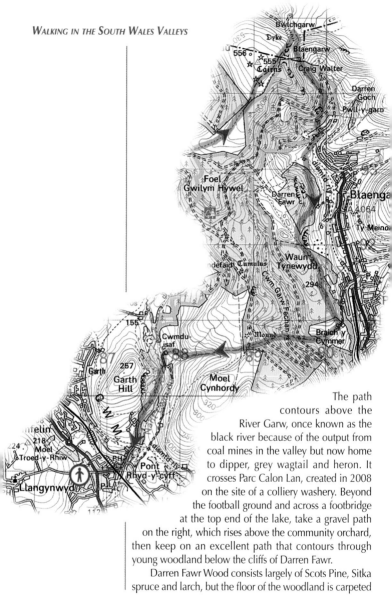

The path contours above the River Garw, once known as the black river because of the output from coal mines in the valley but now home to dipper, grey wagtail and heron. It crosses Parc Calon Lan, created in 2008 on the site of a colliery washery. Beyond the football ground and across a footbridge at the top end of the lake, take a gravel path on the right, which rises above the community orchard, then keep on an excellent path that contours through young woodland below the cliffs of Darren Fawr.

Darren Fawr Wood consists largely of Scots Pine, Sitka spruce and larch, but the floor of the woodland is carpeted

The head of the Garw Valley

with bilberry in the summer months and butterflies such as speckled wood are common here. A path on the right leads up to a viewpoint below the cliffs, but the main route lies south; it is important to take an uphill turn after a few minutes (confirmed by a red waymarker after 200m). The path rises relentlessly, before joining a broader track, crossing a stile and emerging onto the open hillside just above a flagpole erected as a memorial to a local soldier. There are fine views here down into and across the Garw Valley, with Pontycymmer Lake in the foreground.

The route now lies past the former waste tips of Ffaldau Colliery – almost completely erased from the landscape, with just a few steel cables hinting at the aerial ropeway that conveyed the colliery waste here – and over a stile into woodland, eventually reaching the ruins of old stone forestry huts. Near the huts the way-marked path turns left, downhill, but instead follow the rising path southwards, eventually taking a left turn at a crossroads of narrow paths and dropping down to **Braich y Cymmer**, where a well-worn bridleway comes up from the left. Turn right along this, passing through fields and then woodland, and dropping down to reach another forest track. Turn right here, then left on a narrow path that descends to cross the Garw Fechan on a solid wooden footbridge, before climbing steadily up to Croes y Bwlch Gwyn.

Go straight across the ridge-top track, taking a faint path across a field and then swinging left onto a superb old green lane, with Nant y Fforest down to the left in a little gorge. The lane winds through Cwmdu Isaf Farm, and then follows the stream again, with broadleaved woodland, including willow, ash and alder, to the right. Keep ahead under a spectacular viaduct, which once carried coal trains on the Port Talbot railway, and then go past the Tylers Arms and cross the Llynfi River to reach Station Road and finally the main Llynfi valley road at **Pont Rhyd-y-cyff**. Garth station lies around half a mile (0.8km) to the right along this road.

WALK 11
The Glamorgan Ridgeway

Start	Margam Park (SS 802 863)
Finish	Caerphilly Castle (ST 155 870)
Distance	27 miles (43km)
Public transport	Bus X1 provides an hourly service between Bridgend, Margam, Port Talbot and Swansea. Buses 21 and 22 provide a frequent service from Blackmill to Bridgend. Llantrisant has an hourly service (244) to Pontypridd and Bridgend, with connections to Cardiff. Caerphilly has four trains an hour to Cardiff.
Accommodation	If you plan to tackle the route in three stages, as described here, with overnight stops, the accommodation options are currently very limited but this is likely to improve as the route becomes better known. At the time of writing, the only convenient option in Blackmill is Heron's Brook guest house (Tel 01656 849450) but a wider choice is available in Bridgend. A couple of the pubs in Llantrisant offer bed and breakfast – try the Cross Keys (Tel 01443 222155) or the New Inn (Tel 01443 222232). The Three Saints (Tel 01443 222386) and a Premier Inn (Tel 0871 527 8640) are located on the northern outskirts of the town.

The Glamorgan Ridgeway is a user-friendly amalgamation of two former waymarked paths, the Ogwr Ridgeway and Ffordd y Bryniau, which previously met rather unhelpfully in remote moorland on Mynydd y Gaer.

The deer park boundary at Margam Park

Now the complete walk can be tackled in three logical and easily accessible stages, allowing walkers to savour the experience of traversing the most southerly ridges of the valleys, with wide views over the coastal plains.

There is a series of attractive summits, such as Mynydd Baeden, the Garth Mountain and Craig yr Allt, to be conquered.

STAGE 1
Margam Park to Blackmill

Start	Margam Park (SS 802 863)
Finish	Blackmill (SS 933 867)
Distance	10 miles (16km)
Ascent	520m (1705ft)
Time	4–6hrs
Map(s)	Explorer 151, 165, 166

The outstanding feature of this energetic ridge walk, the first stage of a 27-mile (43km) marathon, is the variety of scenery encountered along the way. There is a vivid contrast between the rugged, incised valley and the wealth of historic landmarks, including the abbey, orangery and parkland of Margam, and the house platforms of the medieval settlement on Mynydd Ty-talwyn.

Take the track leading from **Margam** mansion through the deer park gates and around the east side of Mynydd y Castell, with its Iron Age promontory fort. Head eastwards, climbing steadily on a rough track that runs above the Breast

Map continues on page 88

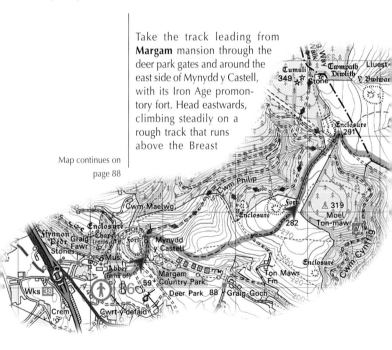

Plantations (a prominent landmark from the M4 away towards the coast) and passes the Bro stone, erected to celebrate the area's close-knit communities.

The orangery at Margam Park

The **Margam** area has a quite astonishing array of landscape features. There is an Iron Age hillfort, a ruined Cistercian abbey, a huge 19th-century mock-Tudor mansion and a stunning Georgian orangery and citrus house in Palladian style. All are set within sylvan parkland, which also includes a walled deer park, pleasure grounds and kitchen garden. The abbey, whose 12th-century nave survives, controlled vast estates through a system of grange farms. Much of the surrounding landscape owes its present form to monastic cattle and sheep-rearing in medieval times.

A track on the line of the prehistoric routeway from Margam to the Llynfi Valley leaves the deer park over a high metal stile. It becomes a splendid sunken green lane, running to the right of a post-and-wire fence, and leads past a barely discernible Iron Age earthwork to reach a crossroads of dirt tracks above the forest edge. Route-finding is crucial here, especially in a landscape that has opened out dramatically in recent times from substantial clear-felling.

Go straight ahead, ignoring the stile leading left, and curve around the head of the flat-bottomed valley of Cwm Cynffig at Rhyd Blaen-y-cwm. A forest road goes south-east, but it is vital to leave this to the left after around 400m, at a signpost without waymarks, crossing a field with a post-and-wire forest boundary fence to the right (the trees have gone as the whole area was recently clear-felled). After 100m, there is a broken-down stile with a gate close by. Go through the gate and immediately swing right, still in company with the forest fence, on a clear track across grassy moorland. The Severn Estuary lies to the right, while to the left are the hills of upland Glamorgan, behind the ancient village of Llangynwyd with its striking whitewashed church.

The track narrows and heads straight towards a junction of minor roads. Take the lane leading straight on. ◀

The Ridgeway passes to the north of the low rounded hill of **Mynydd Ty-talwyn**. This is now an upland sheep-walk but there are traces of former human occupation, including several platform

There are fleeting views down to the left of Gadlys, the home farm of an important post-medieval estate with its own bakehouse and brewery.

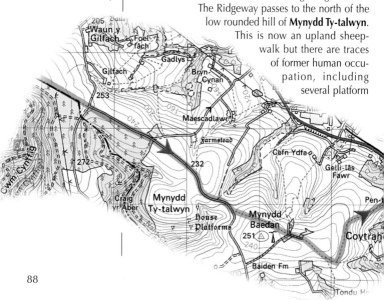

houses and associated field systems and pillow mounds – artificial rabbit warrens constructed to provide a supplement to a restricted medieval diet. A proposed windfarm may have an effect but, for the moment, the views from the lane are sensational, both northwards to the open moorland across the Llynfi Valley, and south-west down the deeply incised valley of the Nant Fadog, with its bracken-covered slopes, over the forested Craig yr Aber to the coastal plain beyond.

Just beyond the distinctive wooded valley of Cwm Nant-gwyn, the ridgeway leaves the road to the left, now on a path that crosses the northern slopes of Mynydd Baeden – said to be the site of King Arthur's last battle – and then swings north-east as it descends rapidly into the Llynfi Valley. It crosses the trackbed of the former Duffryn, Llynvi and Porthcawl railway (actually a horse-drawn tramroad) and then the main road, railway and, finally, the river north of **Coytrahen**. The route then snakes through fields and woodland past Nant-mwth-fawr as it negotiates the low ridge separating the Llynfi and Garw rivers.

The route zigzags left and right across Betws Road, running alongside bungalows and then down a lane that skirts the melancholy remains of the once-impressive country house of Plas-y-Betws. ▶

The fortified manor house, which dates from the 16th century and was built on the site of one of the granges of Margam Abbey, had a remarkable Tudor garden.

The northern slopes of Mynydd Baeden

The track, worn down to the bedrock in places, veers right past Cwm-y-pandy, a little hamlet which had a tannery, corn mill, two spinsters' cottages and a fulling mill, at the time when Plas-y-Betws was at its height. It crosses the fast-flowing River Garw – also known as the 'harsh river', but one that supports varied bird life including kingfisher, dipper and grey wagtail, together with mink and otters.

The ridgeway now climbs past the farms at Cefnmachen-uchaf and Blaenclydwyn, before another descent follows, above delightful oak woodlands with a rich array of wildlife and plants, to **Blackmill** in the Ogmore Valley. This was once an important junction on the railways, taking coal to the Bristol Channel sea ports, and is now a quiet suburban village close to the bustling town of Bridgend.

STAGE 2
Blackmill to Llantrisant

Start	Blackmill (SS 933 867)
Finish	Llantrisant (ST 047 835)
Distance	8 miles (13km)
Ascent	350m (1150ft)
Time	4–5hrs
Map(s)	Explorer 151, 166

This second section of the Glamorgan Ridgeway provides a very varied walking experience, taking in the open moorland of Mynydd y Gaer and Mynydd Maendy, the thickly wooded Llantrisant Forest, and the ruined castle, cobbled streets and historic town centre of Llantrisant. The isolated ruins of St Peter's Church, wholly unexpected in their ridge-top setting, provide added historical interest.

From the A4061 at Blackmill, a steady climb gains the ridge at Caner Bach, with the Blackmill oak woodlands seen below during the ascent. The route then meanders across Waun Wen and swings east, making for the col north of Cwm Llwyd (a substantial Iron Age hillfort sits on a south-facing spur above the valley here, overlooking much more recent mine workings). The route lies south of the summit of **Mynydd y Gaer**,

Map continues on page 92

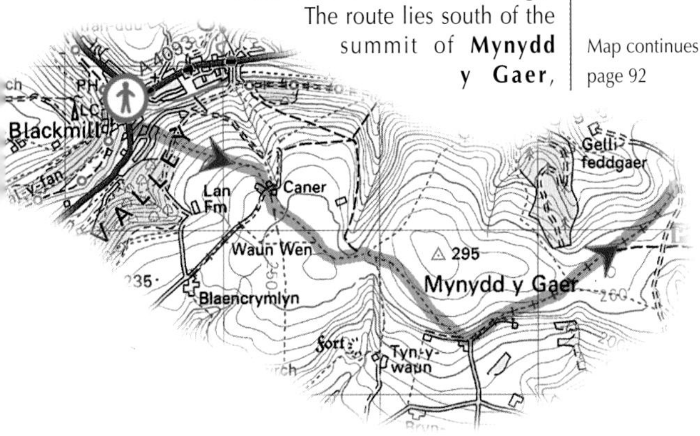

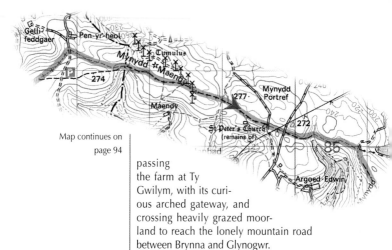

Map continues on
page 94

passing
the farm at Ty
Gwilym, with its curi-
ous arched gateway, and
crossing heavily grazed moorland to reach the lonely mountain road
between Brynna and Glynogwr.

Take the obvious track heading eastwards across the
common, with the Taff Ely windfarm on **Mynydd Maendy**
already dominating the view. ◄

The track drops down easily to reach a gate, and then
climbs on grass between low banks; a notice asks walkers to keep to the parish road, an indication both of the
route's antiquity and of the desire to keep walkers away
from the wind turbines strung along the ridge.

Follow the clear but sometimes damp track through
several more gates between the easterly turbines, and
down to a col with a fine view through the hills to the
left to the conspicuous landmark of Tylorstown Tip on the
horizon. The ridgeway continues as an enclosed lane,
with the substantial remains of St Peter's Super Montem
already visible on the right; eventually a gate gives access
to this remarkable site.

One of the earliest
wind farms in Britain,
Taff Ely's 20 turbines
have been operating
since 1993. Their
maximum output is
able to supply the
needs of only 4000
homes.

> The ruins of **St Peter's Church**, remarkable both for
> their exposed upland location and their extent, date
> from the 13th century, but excavations have shown
> that there was a fifth- or sixth-century Celtic 'bee-
> hive' hermitage here, and possibly an even earlier
> Christian site. The jury is still out, however, on the
> extraordinary theory that earthworks close to the
> church are the site of the legendary Caer Caradog,

The ruins of St Peter's Church

supposedly a rectangular walled city that existed before the arrival of the Romans and that is also alleged to be associated with King Arthur.

Return to the enclosed lane, crossing the old road from Brynna to the Rhondda Valleys, with the woodland cloaking Mynydd Garthmaelwg now in view ahead. The ridgeway path is clearly marked as it meanders through the plantation close to a group of round barrows known as The Beacons, gradually losing height as the route approaches the Ely Valley. Turn right upon reaching a minor road near **Ynysmaerdy**, and then take a sharp turn left onto a path that crosses a disused railway and takes a path just south of the Royal Glamorgan Hospital boundary fence.

The path heads towards and then crosses a dual carriageway (extreme care is needed here) and slants up a lane before climbing onto the common land of Y Graig, now on a superb green path (though disappointingly out of sight of the disused 14th-century windmill, restored as a folly by the Victorians). The path enters the interesting little town of **Llantrisant** along a little lane, zigzags right and left into Yr Allt, an appealingly cobbled street, and turns right

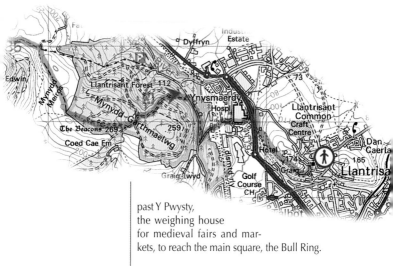

past Y Pwysty,
the weighing house
for medieval fairs and mar-
kets, to reach the main square, the Bull Ring.

Llantrisant, or the 'town of three saints' is the home
of the Royal Mint and perhaps inevitably is known
as 'the hole with the mint'. Little remains of the
castle, and the church is heavily restored, but the
Model House, which now houses craft workshops,
was once the union workhouse and then successively a boarding house, an inn, a general store
and finally a glove factory. The Bull Ring contains
a statue of the eccentric surgeon and druid Dr
William Price, a pioneer of cremation.

*Mynydd
Garthmaelwg from
Y Graig*

STAGE 3
Llantrisant to Caerphilly Castle

Start	Llantrisant (ST 047 835)
Finish	Caerphilly Castle (ST 155 870)
Distance	9 miles (14km)
Ascent	645m (2115ft)
Time	4–6hrs
Map(s)	Explorer 151, 166

This last section of the Glamorgan Ridgeway is a bit of a misnomer, as it deserts the high ground to cross the broad valley of the Nant Myddlin and then the River Taff, but it includes some superb ridge walking across Garth Mountain, Craig yr Allt and Caerphilly Mountain. It ends at the magnificent, moated Caerphilly Castle, the largest stronghold in Wales, with its concentric walls, leaning tower, and series of moats.

Leave **Llantrisant** along Erw Hir, forking right onto a clear path just before the last few houses and contouring along the ridge. Dip down after a kissing gate to turn right at a disused railway line and immediately reach the old main road, now a cycleway alongside the Church Village bypass. Follow this for some 500m, then cross the bypass on the bridge carrying the access road to Rhiwbrwdwal Farm.

Map continues on page 96

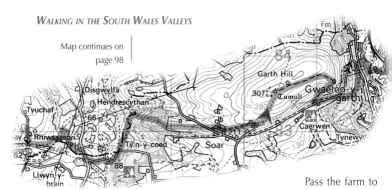

Map continues on page 98

The fort is the alleged site of the Battle of Rhiwsaeson between the Saxons and the Welsh in AD873.

Garth Mountain from Ty-mawr Farm

Pass the farm to the right, go through a gate and join a path leading through a delightful copse and then passing below the imposing northern ramparts of Caerau hillfort, its enormous central enclosure protected by two banks and ditches. The original entrance was to the south-east, with a narrow passageway between parallel inturned banks. ◄

Route-finding is a little tricky on the next section! The path leads through drifts of bluebells in spring to a track; turn left here to a minor road at Ty-mawr Farm,

then right along the road and left onto a track just before an old railway bridge. When the track is confronted by a raised pipeline, go left to a gateway, cross the next field (the key is to locate an elaborate footbridge over a minor stream) and through two more, to emerge next to the Caesar's Arms. Take the first left beyond the pub, following the lane until it bends sharply right at the Forestry Commission's Ty'n-y-coed car park.

Take the pleasant and obvious track through the woods, skirting the base of Craig Gwilym, at first across level ground but then rather surprisingly climbing quite steeply past evidence of old mines and quarries. Ignore three paths going to the left. Height is gained relentlessly until the track emerges onto an excellent grassy ridge with good views of Garth Mountain and the hills across the Taff Valley. Beyond a couple of unexpected picnic tables the path reaches the lane through the hamlet of **Soar**. ▸

Climb some steps on the left to reach a gravelled track heading for the summit of the Garth, quickly acquiring superb views of Cardiff, the cliffs of Penarth Head and the Severn Estuary. Beyond Ty'n y Ffald, the route quite easily gains the summit ridge, with its assortment of Bronze Age tumuli.

Formerly a mining community, Soar contains ruined miners' cottages and the remains of the former Pentyrch poor houses.

> At 307m (1007ft), **the Garth** hardly qualifies as a mountain but it rises imposingly on the west side of the Taff gorge and starred as the eminence in the film *The Englishman Who Went Up a Hill and Came Down a Mountain*.

Go past three tumuli and a toposcope, then, as the ground suddenly falls away into the Taff gorge, swing sharply right, descending steeply past rocky outcrops to gain a narrow path heading for a narrow lane. Turn left along the lane, then right through a kissing gate, dropping down through woodland to reach the little village of **Gwaelod-y-Garth**.

Just past the Gwaelod-y-Garth Inn, turn right on a path that leads via steps and a subway to a bridge over the Taff. At the main road, the simplest option is to turn left, then right, shortly after Fagin's Ale and Chop House onto Moy Road, following this above the A470 dual carriageway and then turning into Parish Road. Turn left just before a café, and then left again after a few yards onto a tarmac track on the route of a disused railway line. Follow this until the Taff Trail comes in from the right; it is crucial here to turn back towards Cardiff on the Taff Trail, then take the path on the left after 300m, which climbs the lower slopes of Craig yr Allt.

This last section of the Ridgeway is among the best. After a sharp climb there is a terrific view back across the Taff Valley to Garth Mountain; its rocky south-east profile is seen at its best from this angle. On reaching the summit ridge, the surprisingly craggy southern slopes of **Craig yr Allt** itself come into view. A fine sandy path provides exhilarating walking across the top, before a steep descent to reach a minor road at Waun-waelod. Go right, then turn left and cross two fields before climbing again, quickly reaching the open access land of Caerphilly Common.

One of the largest – and finest – medieval castles in Western Europe,

Caerphilly
Castle was begun in 1268 and took around 10 years to complete. The outer ward was formidable enough but the

Caerphilly Castle and its leaning south-east tower

inner ward, entered through a massively imposing gatehouse, was almost impregnable (and indeed withstood a siege by Llewellyn Bren in 1316). The remains are extensive and sensational, not least the south-east tower, which is tilted at an even greater angle than the leaning tower of Pisa.

Easy walking across the common, heading north-east but just below the summit, and skirting the little enclosure at Cwmwbwb, brings the B4600 underfoot. This was once the main road into **Caerphilly** and even though it is quieter now it makes for underwhelming walking. Fortunately, it leads directly to the iconic Caerphilly Castle and the end of the Glamorgan Ridgeway.

3 THE EASTERN RIDGES

Beech woodlands on the Rhymney Valley Ridgeway (Walk 13)

WALK 12
Over the Bwlch

Start	Treorchy station (SS 958 964)
Finish	Llangeinor church (SS 925 879)
Distance	10 miles (16km)
Ascent	385m (1260ft)
Time	4–5hrs
Map(s)	Explorer 166
Public transport	Treorchy has two trains an hour from Cardiff via Pontypridd. A footpath leads steeply down in 600m from Llangeinor church to the A4061, where there is a bus stop and three buses an hour to Bridgend.

Part of the marathon Sky to Sea route from the Cynon Valley across the Rhondda Valleys to the Heritage Coast, this is a challenging walk across high moorland. The compensation is the superb scenery, including the magnificent vista from Craig Ogwr's cliffs down the valley of the Ogwr Fawr to the Bristol Channel and Exmoor. The walk passes the Iron Age hillfort on Mynydd Maendy and uses the old drove road from Werfa Mountain down to the village of Llangeinor.

Take the road south from **Treorchy** station, around a sharp left-hand bend. Quickly turn uphill onto a pleasant woodland path. Go straight across the main road and up a broad, shady forest track, crossing a forest road and emerging onto the open hillside just below a telecoms mast. Go to the left

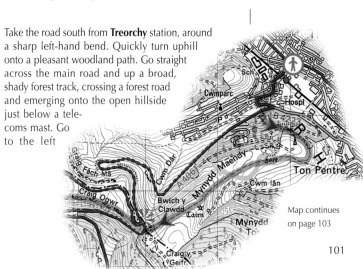

Map continues on page 103

of the mast, savouring the panoramic views of the upper Rhondda Valleys, and curve round to the right to meet a broad track coming up from Ton Pentre.

The track leads up to the low, bracken-covered earthworks of Maendy Camp, an extensive Iron Age hillfort, making good use of the steeply sloping ground at the end of the ridge. ◄

Maendy Camp is lightly defended, with a rubble bank and an external ditch, although the eastern end is sub-divided and has a second earthen bank.

Beyond the fort, the track crosses open grassy moorland, with the huge glacial corrie of Cwm Tair-nant, backed by the towering cliffs of Graig Fawr, around 150m (500ft) high, dominating the scene on the right. A short, steep climb improves the views still further, with the Brecon Beacons now on the northern horizon.

A level walk across the moorland leads to **Bwlch y Clawdd**, a meeting point of high mountain roads. Go straight across, climbing towards the first of the little craggy outcrops of Craig Ogwr, a superb mountain cliff at the head of the Ogwr Fawr Valley. To the south of the valley, with its wooded flanks, the eye is drawn to the coastal plain, the Severn Estuary and the Exmoor hills. Away to the west are the masts close to the summit of Werfa – a useful waymark for the next hour or so.

The Ogwr Fawr Valley from Craig Ogwr

Known locally simply as 'the Bwlch', and named after the eighth century clawdd or dyke lying just to the east, **Bwlch y Clawdd** is the highest point on an A road in Britain. The road was built in the 1930s as an unemployment relief project, while the dyke checked progress along the ancient ridgeway route out of the Rhondda Valleys. An ice cream van is usually in place at the summit car park, and sheep roam the road in search of unwanted food.

Map continues on page 104

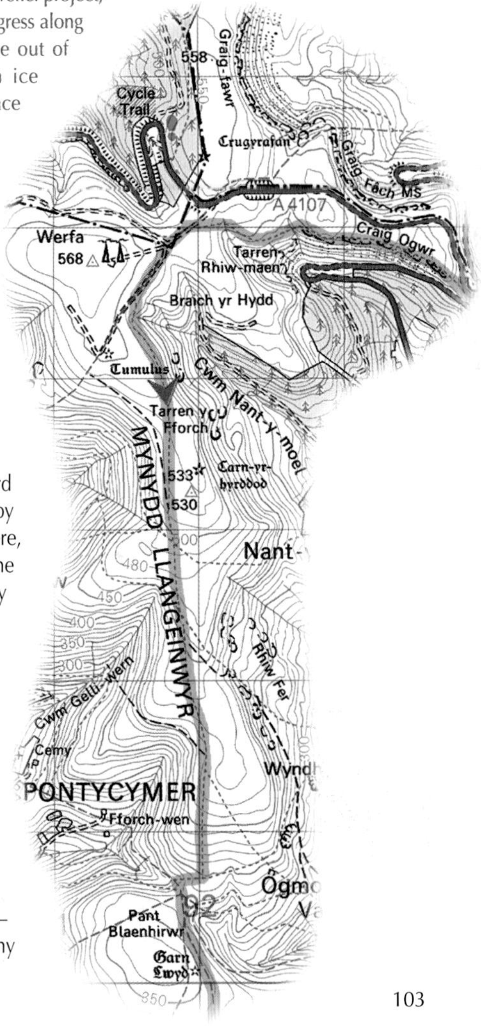

The walk along the ridge above Craig Ogwr is utterly exhilarating, with views between the crags into the Ogwr Fawr Valley. Eventually, the path trends to the right as it dips down to cross the headwaters of the river, via a rocky ford and then a rather more swampy area. The route is ill-defined here, although the key is to aim to the right of the masts, eventually reaching a gate and nearby stile quite close to the road. This dips down into the well-wooded upper Afan Valley, which suddenly appears to the right.

Turn left at the gate onto the concrete track heading for the masts and transmitter station on **Werfa**, cross a cattle grid – wild ponies often congregate here – and immediately take the stony

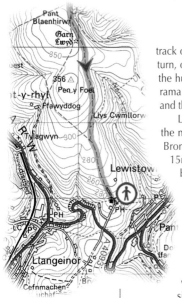

track on the left. It is crucial to take a further left turn, onto a green path heading due south across the huge grassy sheepwalk. A spectacular panorama opens up of the green Vale of Glamorgan and the Severn Estuary beyond.

Landmarks are few and far between on the next section of the route, although the low Bronze Age burial mound of Carn-yr-hyrddod, 15m in diameter and about a metre high, can be discerned to the left just before a fairly random trig point on the declining ridge. To the right lies the Garw Valley, to the left the Ogwr Fawr, although the old mining villages lining the valley floors are rarely in view. The broad grassy ridge of Mynydd Llangeinwr dominates the scene ahead; mixed farming is practised here, with a surprising number of cattle alongside the inevitable sheep, and cotton grass and occasional bilberries.

Above Ogmore Vale, the map suggests that the southward path zigzags to right and left, but this is a fiction: the track drops sharply down to a col and heads straight across. There is a confusing array of tracks here, so keep slightly left, still heading south and climbing steadily to

The drove road approaching Llangeinor

pass the trig point on **Pen y Foel**, the final hill on the walk. There is an excellent retrospective view of the ridge climbing to Werfa from here, while to the south-east the windfarm on Mynydd Maendy is prominent across the broad valley of the Ogwr Fach.

Beyond a gate, the moorland track quickly becomes a delightful walled lane, broadening out to become more recognisably a drove road – it was once called Ffordd-y-Claddwyr, the 'road of the trench-digger', the name betraying another former use as a burial road – which leads through another gate into the ancient heart of the hilltop village of Llangeinor, with St Cein's Church (or Ceinwyr) and the village pub sharing commanding views of the surrounding countryside.

WALK 13

The Rhymney Valley Ridgeway

Start	Traveller's Rest, Caerphilly Mountain (ST 157 843)
Finish	Machen (ST 211 892)
Distance	8 miles (13km)
Ascent	180m (590ft)
Time	3–4hrs
Map(s)	Explorer 151, 152, 166
Public transport	Buses A, B and X provide a half-hourly service between Cardiff, the Traveller's Rest and Caerphilly. Machen is served every 30 minutes by bus 50 between Caerphilly and Newport.

The Rhymney Valley Ridgeway Walk is a varied 28-mile (45km) circuit of the hills surrounding the Caerphilly Basin. This excerpt follows the most enjoyable section, along the ridge between Caerphilly and the coastal plain, with the opportunity to explore castles (notably the atmospheric ruin of Ruperra Castle), ancient woodlands and industrial remains.

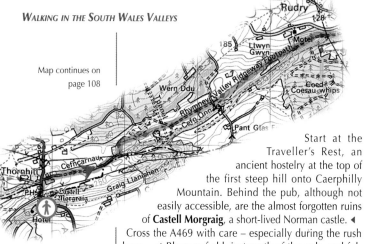

Map continues on
page 108

Start at the Traveller's Rest, an ancient hostelry at the top of the first steep hill onto Caerphilly Mountain. Behind the pub, although not easily accessible, are the almost forgotten ruins of **Castell Morgraig**, a short-lived Norman castle. ◄

Cross the A469 with care – especially during the rush hour – at Blaen-nofydd, just north of the pub, and follow the well-defined track climbing between woodland and farmland. Zigzag left and then right, now walking through fine beech woodland, with a spectacular panorama northwards of wooded hills across the Rhymney Valley.

A curiosity next: the map shows the bridleway going straight ahead through a quarry. Instead, veer slightly to the left to avoid the cliffs, but not before taking in the fine views through the green-floored quarry entrance to the Severn Estuary. The ridgeway keeps straight on through farmland to reach a minor road at the sprawling **Cefn-onn Farm**, before skirting woodland (an iron cable accompanies the path for several hundred metres) and then dropping down steeply to cross a stile at a junction of paths.

The descent continues, through the mixed woodland of Coed Coesau-whips on the flank of Craig y Llyn, close to the site of a hitherto secret World War II bunker, which was revealed to the public in 2011. ◄

Just before reaching the Maen Llwyd pub in **Rudry**, the route turns sharply right on a forest track and then left to reach a road junction. Take the right-hand of two virtually parallel bridleways, passing Coed y Squire and suddenly reaching the substantial remains of **Ruperra Castle**. It is worth taking a detour on the right just before

Built around 1243, Castell Morgraig was abandoned, unfinished, in 1267, when the de Clare family defeated the last local Welsh native chieftain and began to build the much grander Caerphilly Castle.

The bunker, probably used by the auxiliary units as a radio contact point, is protected by fencing, but there is a good view down the main shaft and into the partially collapsed main chamber.

the castle, on a path alongside the wall, which has several views of the striking facade.

> The ruined **Ruperra Castle**, built for Sir Thomas Morgan in 1626, presents a forlorn sight these days. Roofless since a major fire in 1942, which also accounted for one of the four corner towers, it was a stylish early Renaissance house, battlemented and with Gothic windows. It stands in derelict formal gardens and is surrounded by manicured parkland.

Just beyond the main entrance to the castle, take a path on the left, initially climbing a flight of steps and then reaching a crossroads of paths. Turn right here on a superb grassy path cresting the ridge, with views back to the castle at one point, before arriving at the remains of the summerhouse on the eastern tip of Coed Craig Ruperra.

> **Coed Craig Ruperra** is a magical place, used and reused for thousands of years. It has an Iron Age fort

Ruperra Castle from Craig Ruperra

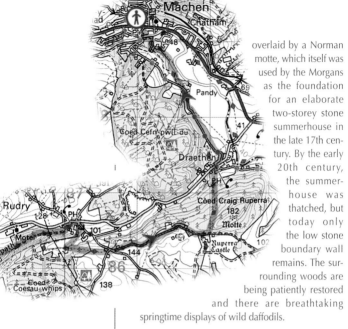

overlaid by a Norman motte, which itself was used by the Morgans as the foundation for an elaborate two-storey stone summerhouse in the late 17th century. By the early 20th century, the summerhouse was thatched, but today only the low stone boundary wall remains. The surrounding woods are being patiently restored and there are breathtaking springtime displays of wild daffodils.

The motte and summerhouse at Coed Craig Ruperra

Return to the junction of paths and turn right, walking through open woodland and emerging on a wide track that winds down to a gate at the edge of the woodland. Cross a large field, with the dormitory village of **Draethen** in the valley ahead. Go straight across the main road, taking a footpath and then a lane on the edge of Coed Cefn-pwll-du, with the remains of ancient lead mines, some allegedly dating back to Roman times, running up the hillside on the left. Just beyond Rhyd-y-Gwern Farm, take a path on the right, just above the river. Across the valley lies Machen corn mill, with a derelict mill house, brick chimney and traces of the millrace, while across a footbridge spanning the River Rhymney the walk ends at the village of **Machen** itself.

WALK 14

Above the upper Rhymney

Start	Hengoed station (ST 153 949)
Finish	Bute Town (SO 103 091)
Distance	13 miles (21km)
Ascent	465m (1525ft)
Time	5–7hrs
Map(s)	Explorer 166, Outdoor Leisure 13
Public transport	Hengoed has four trains an hour from Cardiff; Bute Town is 1¼ miles (2km) from Rhymney, on the same line but with only an hourly service.

Once billed as an extension to the Rhymney Valley Ridgeway Walk but no longer promoted as such, this is an invigorating excursion across hidden farmland and high moorland, often with inspiring views ahead of the Brecon Beacons, ending at one of the most surprising locations of the industrial revolution in Wales. The walk visits the remains of Roman forts and practice works, two abandoned moorland chapels and an early 19th-century model village.

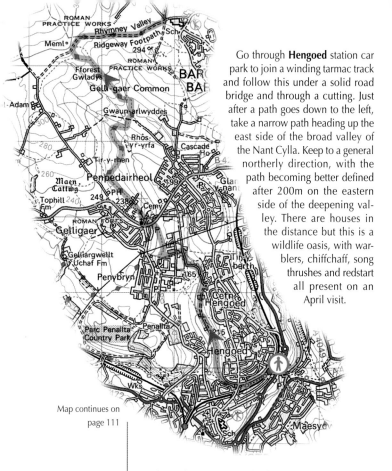

Go through **Hengoed** station car park to join a winding tarmac track and follow this under a solid road bridge and through a cutting. Just after a path goes down to the left, take a narrow path heading up the east side of the broad valley of the Nant Cylla. Keep to a general northerly direction, with the path becoming better defined after 200m on the eastern side of the deepening valley. There are houses in the distance but this is a wildlife oasis, with warblers, chiffchaff, song thrushes and redstart all present on an April visit.

Map continues on page 111

The path runs between hedges and a wire fence and eventually joins a roughly surfaced private road. Follow this uphill through a curious mix of horsiculture and spoil heaps. Turn left along a winding country lane, which has been blocked off and is slowly being reclaimed by nature. Veer left onto a good path at the end of the blocked section, then cross a road in the middle of an industrial estate before plunging straight back onto a wooded path. Turn right across a new footbridge to take an enclosed path emerging in the middle of **Gelligaer**, which features a church, chapel, pub and post office. Go past the church onto a path signposted as the 'Roman walk' across fields to two Roman forts.

Map continues on page 113

The substantial stone-built **Gelligaer Roman fort**, constructed in the early second century and capable of garrisoning 500 men, must have presented an extraordinary sight when it was excavated in the early 20th century: barracks, a parade ground, a bath house, a granary and a pottery were all uncovered. Both this substantial fort and its earth and timber predecessor a little to the north-west, built at the time of the Roman conquest of Wales only 30 years earlier, lie under grassland now. Their sites are discernible only as raised platforms in adjacent fields.

Beyond the second fort, head straight across two fields and turn right on a track, then left through a metal kissing gate and around the next field to a further gate and

Groes-faen and the Darran Valley

a footbridge. Take a curving course, well signposted, across four fields to reach the open moorland of Gelligaer Common. Turn right to cross the stream at a ford, then left to follow the track across the common to a minor road. The walk across the common is delightful, on firm grass and with the song of numerous skylarks for company in spring and summer.

Across the minor road, the cross marking the site of Capel Gwladys is prominently in view. ◄

St Gwladys, mother of St Cadoc, came to live here as a hermit around AD500, while an inscribed stone slab found on the site dates to the ninth century.

Follow the road eastwards across the common, passing the site of Roman practice works. At least six practice camps, the products of military exercises, can be found on Gelligaer Common, marked by low banks and ditches. Continue along the road, now with an outstanding view on the left of the heavily wooded Darran Valley, then at a road junction go left over a cattle grid and immediately take a bridleway, with a golf course beyond a wall on the right.

The bridleway quickly becomes an enjoyable green path, which angles steeply down to cross the Bargoed Rhymney River and curves round to pass under an old railway bridge in company with the river. A track heads steeply up to reach the hamlet of Groes-faen, then the route continues northwards on a splendid bridleway, which takes the form of a walled lane north of Groes-faen Farm, then emerges onto a hilltop sheepwalk. Zigzag right and then left around a huge field, before taking a superb green lane between vestigial stone walls, with sylvan countryside ahead (except for the grassed-over spoil heaps on the skyline beyond the Nant Llan Valley).

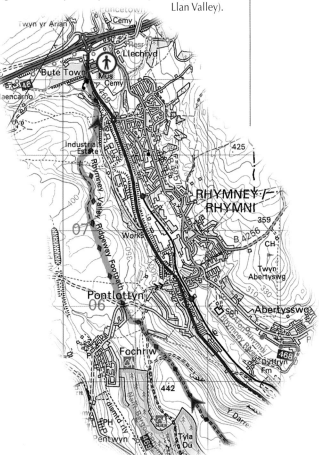

The next section is one of the highlights of the walk, along a glorious green lane through forgotten countryside, which appears to have seen few changes for centuries. Nothing disturbs the peace except birdsong – including the distinctive yaffling call of the green woodpecker. Drop down to cross the Nant Llan stream, then climb steeply up another walled green lane – its floor is a carpet of celandines in spring – to join a narrow tarmac lane at Ty'r Capel.

Turn left when the road bends right; the Celtic cross on the site of Capel y Brithdir quickly comes into view on the right. ◄

Just beyond the chapel, a plain stone in a field on the left of the track marks the former location of the Tegernacus Stone, a massive inscribed slab, possibly dating from the seventh century, which was moved to the National Museum of Wales in 1922. The inscription was 'Tegernacus, son of Martius, lies here', but there is no sign of a burial mound or any other feature.

The eerie ridge-top graveyard survives, but the chapel, repaired in the 1730s, was ruinous again a century later. In the late 19th century, there was a rotten wooden belfry but no bell, since this had been stolen in 1858.

Capel y Brithdir with the Tegernacus Stone beyond

For the next hour the walking is exhilarating, following an old ridgeway route along **Cefn y Brithdir**, with the glorious Brecon Beacons landscape directly ahead and aerial views into and across the upper Rhymney Valley. Bronze Age cairns and medieval house platforms litter the ridge, an upland heath awash with bilberries in summer. Beyond a telecoms mast, the road contours above Rhiw Cantorion before crossing the mountain road that comes up from Pontlottyn. It is tempting to cut down here to Pontlottyn station, but one more treat awaits those who trek the additional 2 miles (3km) across the open common west of Rhymney – the model village of **Bute Town**. ▶

Remarkably, three rows of cottages, built to a high standard in the 1820s to house workers at the Union Ironworks in Rhymney, have survived. Originally, the village had its own chapel, pub and school.

WALK 15
The Sirhowy Valley

Start	Aneurin Bevan Memorial Stones, Bryn Serth (SO 151 106)
Finish	Argoed (ST 177 998)
Distance	8 miles (13km)
Ascent	235m (770ft)
Time	3–4hrs
Map(s)	Outdoor Leisure 13, Explorer 166
Public transport	Bus X4 (Cardiff to Abergavenny via Merthyr) calls hourly at Bryn Serth near Tredegar. Argoed is served by bus 56, with an hourly service from Tredegar to Newport.

The Sirhowy Valley Walk is a 26-mile (42km) marathon following the valley from the old industrial town of Tredegar to Tredegar House, a country mansion on the outskirts of Newport. This extract uses the initial part of the route, from inauspicious beginnings on the outskirts of Tredegar (a slightly curious setting for the memorial to the 'father of the NHS') over the long, broad ridge of Cefn Manmoel and alongside the river to Cwm-corrwg.

Start at the four solid stones commemorating the life of Aneurin Bevan, in a dramatic and windswept

Born in Tredegar in 1897, Bevan established the National Health Service while minister of health in the post-war Labour government.

setting on **Bryn Serth**. The views northwards are wide and inspiring. ◀ A vivid green path leads to a minor road, passing through woodland and then across common land grazed by ponies to Mountain Air Gate.

Take the track past a Manmoel Common notice board, curving left and then right as it rises towards two TV masts. Tredegar and the Sirhowy Valley are seen to the right, beyond the woodland. This conceals Scotch Peter's reservoir, which was enlarged in the 1950s but abandoned half a century later. The bulky Mynydd Carn-y-cefn fills the eastern horizon.

The track runs just below the crest of the ridge, with open bilberry and heather moorland to the left, a terrific retrospective view of Pen-y-Fan, the highest of the Brecon Beacons, beyond Tredegar, and an equally impressive view down a wooded side valley across **Troedrhiwgwair** to the flat-topped Mynydd Bedwellte on the far side of the Sirhowy Valley. Sadly, the Fountain, a classic farmhouse pub with a meeting room for the Royal & Ancient Order of Buffaloes, closed in 2003.

The Sirhowy Valley from above Troedrhiwgwair

The route traverses the Cruglwyn plateau, with heather moorland, dilapidated drystone walls and a

well-preserved bell pit hinting at a coal mining past. As the view opens out southwards to Mynydd Machen and the hills above Caerphilly, the rough track is replaced by a rather weather-beaten metalled surface and another notice board is encountered, this one with a Sirhowy Valley Walk waymark. The walk heads towards a flat-topped hill, which to the casual observer looks natural but on closer inspection is revealed as a sympathetically landscaped waste tip from the former Marine Colliery, which employed more than 2000 men at Cwm in the Ebbw Valley.

The Sirhowy Valley swings away to the right here and there is an excellent view down the well-wooded Nant-yr-Helyg Valley, with clear-felled woodland on its southern slopes. The walk meets a cattle grid at the edge of the common and immediately leaves the tarmac road, using a waymarked stony track on the right, which runs beneath a shady avenue of mature trees. Turn left on reaching a lane, dropping down to the edge of **Manmoel**, a tranquil village curiously bypassed by the industrial revolution; its most striking feature is perhaps the restored stone-walled village pound.

Take a signposted path on the right, just before entering the village. Cross several fields – the waymarking is exemplary – and reach a stile with a superb view down

Map continues on page 118

the deeply incised, well-wooded Nant y Felin Valley. Turn right here, looking out for buzzards and red kites soaring above **Hafodrisclawdd** Wood (recently opened up to visitors and boasting superb wildlife) on the far side of the valley, and then pass below Ysgubor-newydd to reach a narrow lane by the ruins of Ton-y-groes Farm.

The lane descends to Twyn-gwyn and somewhat abruptly becomes a green track, braiding and then becoming stony as the slope steepens and the track winds down towards the Sirhowy Valley. At a junction, a lane to the right dives even more steeply beneath a dismantled railway, but the walk goes left along a track through woodland and then skirts above Ty'r-graig, now on a narrow track on a bracken-infested hillside.

The head-high bracken can be a trial in high summer, but eventually much more pleasant ground is reached as the path passes through oak woodland on a bench above the unseen Sirhowy. An open area to the right is all that is left of a former colliery; just beyond this, turn left up a shady track, gaining height quickly to go over a metal stile onto a narrow lane.

The views open out here, with the village of Markham incongruously perched on a high bench on the far side of the valley in an otherwise green and well-wooded setting. The lane is level at first, but beyond Pen-deri Farm and its attendant house martins, the gradient steepens markedly, with the Sirhowy River at last coming into view, below and to the right. The route passes beneath the disused railway, then leaves the Sirhowy Valley Walk and turns right and crosses the river on a solid road

Hafodrisclawdd Wood and the Nant y Felin Valley

bridge. Follow the road as it winds through the hamlet of Cwm-corrwg, climbing to reach **Argoed** and the main road from Tredegar to Newport.

WALK 16
Mynydd Carn-y-Cefn and the Round Towers

Start	Cwm Big, Aberbeeg (SO 205 020)
Finish	Nantyglo Round Towers (SO 188 102)
Distance	5½ miles (9km)
Ascent	420m (1380ft)
Time	3–4hrs
Map(s)	Explorer 166, Outdoor Leisure 13
Public transport	Buses E3 and E4 provide a half-hourly service between Aberbeeg and Nantyglo.

This is a serious mountain walk, which climbs steadily between the Ebbw and Ebbw Fach valleys to conquer Mynydd Carn-y-Cefn. At 550m (1804ft), it is one of the highest points in the valleys. There is an eclectic range of sights along the way, from the old brewery vat at Hafod-y-dafal Farm above Aberbeeg, through the beech woodlands of Silent Valley, the chasms on the steep mountain sides, to the Nantyglo Round Towers, the last castle-like fortifications to be constructed in Britain.

Map continues on
page 122

The initial stages of the walk are quite challenging, on a rough and stony path that climbs steeply from the corner of the Cwm Big lay-by, north-west of **Aberbeeg**, through open, airy woodland alongside a dilapidated drystone wall. Beyond a gate at the top of the wood, the path is faint at first, alongside a bank that forms an ancient field boundary, but then it becomes much clearer, crossing upland pastures and rising only very gradually as it approaches the derelict farmhouse of **Hafod-y-dafal**. An old brewery mash tun stands somewhat incongruously in front of the farmhouse. It was relocated here from Webbs Brewery in the valley below, and the current farmer recalls it providing bathing water in the 1950s.

A clear track curves left and then right across the plateau, before leaving the fields of Hafod-y-dafal behind at a gate giving access to the common grazings on the broad ridge of **Cefn yr Arail**. This Pennant Sandstone massif contained valuable coal seams and collieries were established all around it, with adits extending under the mountain and eventually undermining it. There are large landslips on the steep sides, and a series of chasms on the plateau, some fenced off by the Coal Authority but some not, so it is essential to **take care when crossing the plateau**. On the right, the work to reclaim the tip of the Six Bells Colliery – the last big project in the eastern valleys – can be seen on the skyline.

Thankfully, there is a clear green path to follow, at first on the western side of the

The brewery mash tun at Hafod-y-dafal

moorland, with excellent views from above the Silent Valley nature reserve across the Ebbw Valley to the former Garden Festival site beneath Cefn Manmoel. ▶

Back on the ridge, the path continues inexorably northwards, with heather, bilberries and rough grassland supporting huge numbers of ground-nesting birds, including meadow pipits and skylarks, while a small population of red grouse still clings on in the more extensive tracts of heather. The ridge narrows by the head of Cwm Merddog and the path swings across to the eastern edge, now with the Sugar Loaf and the Black Mountains on the horizon. The trig point marking the summit of **Mynydd Carn-y-Cefn** lies some 200m to the left of the path, across tussocky heather moorland; the summit is undistinguished except for the fine all-round panorama.

A thin path leads north across the moor, passing close to the low banks of a Bronze Age cairn above Bwlch y Garn. From here, the descent to Nantyglo is relatively gentle, on a broad track that passes a golf course on the left and then runs between old coal tips, now reclaimed by heather. Turn right here, passing a row of bungalows, to see the Round Towers.

The beech woodlands of Silent Valley are among the most westerly in the UK, and the reserve boasts heath spotted orchids, a variety of mosses and liverworts on the colliery spoil, and a good range of woodland birds.

121

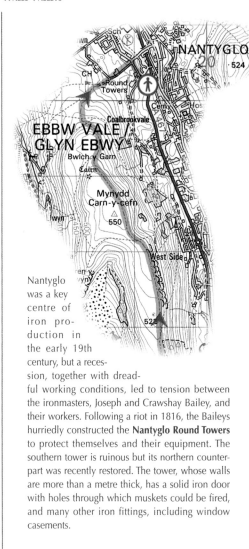

Nantyglo was a key centre of iron production in the early 19th century, but a recession, together with dreadful working conditions, led to tension between the ironmasters, Joseph and Crawshay Bailey, and their workers. Following a riot in 1816, the Baileys hurriedly constructed the **Nantyglo Round Towers** to protect themselves and their equipment. The southern tower is ruinous but its northern counterpart was recently restored. The tower, whose walls are more than a metre thick, has a solid iron door with holes through which muskets could be fired, and many other iron fittings, including window casements.

WALK 17

St Illtyd's and the Guardian of the Valleys

Start	Llanhilleth railway station (SO 216 007)
Finish	Abertillery & District Museum (SO 216 042)
Distance	10 miles (16km)
Ascent	470m (1540ft)
Time	4–6hrs
Map(s)	Explorer 152, Outdoor Leisure 13
Public transport	Llanhilleth has an hourly train service to Cardiff; Abertillery has half-hourly buses to Llanhilleth and Newport.

An early objective of this exhilarating high-level walk is the isolated St Illtyd's Church, with an inn, a castle motte and drovers' tracks for company. The ridge route follows one of these tracks over high moorland, before dipping down to Blaentillery Farm at the head of the Tyleri Valley. The walk finishes at Abertillery, just above Six Bells, now home of the 'Guardian of the Valleys', a stunning memorial to the colliery disaster.

From **Llanhilleth** station, turn left along the main road. Just after passing the rugby club, look for a flight of steps next to a dilapidated chapel; climb the steps and then zigzag steeply up the hillside on a tarmac path. Cross two roads, using lanes to reach the access road to the Penrhiwfer estate. Take this road through the estate, turning right at the end and then immediately left to go through a gate onto a delightful green path on a sylvan bench, already with an imposing view of the wooded hills and deeply incised valleys around Aberbeeg.

A muddy track skirts the farm at Argoed, high

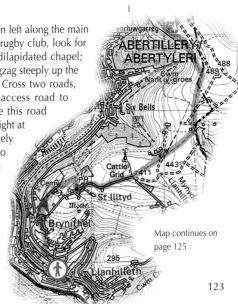

Map continues on page 125

123

St Illtyd's Church, Llanhilleth

above the Ebbw Fach Valley and just above the cemetery where the victims of the Six Bells Colliery disaster were buried. The going improves across two fields, before an awkward stile gives access to a patch of scrubby woodland. Turn right at the far side of the enclosure, cross another awkward stile, and head diagonally up through a field that contains the remains of Castell Taliorum, a short-lived stone-built 14th-century structure, to **St Illtyd's Church**.

> There has reputedly been a church on this site since the fifth century, although much of the present fabric of **St Illtyd's Church** dates from when it was rebuilt by the Cistercians 700 years later. Nearby opencast coal mining badly affected the fabric of the church during the 20th century, and it was closed and deconsecrated in 1957. Renovated by the Friends of St Illtyd, it remains an evocative site in its roughly circular churchyard on a lonely hilltop.

A short detour south leads to the motte of an earlier Llanhilleth Castle, apparently destroyed in the 13th century; but the route lies northwards, past the Carpenters Arms and along the mountain road to Abersychan. Leave this road just after a cattle grid, taking a broad and, in places, badly rutted track across Llanhilleth Mountain common, passing Ty Dafydd and skirting sheep pens. A wide track continues ahead, alongside a wall. There is a sensational view down the steep-sided valley of Cwm Nant-y-Groes to the former mining settlement of Six Bells,

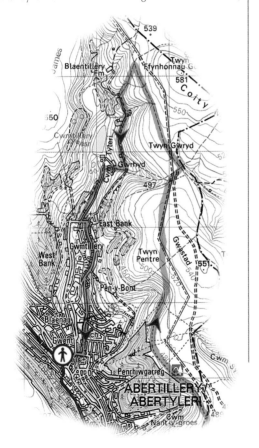

The path alongside Cwmtillery reservoir

with the statue of the 'Guardian' conspicuous on the far side of the Ebbw Fach River.

Originally opened in 1892 as Arael Griffin Colliery, **Six Bells** once employed around 3000 miners. In June 1960, an explosion, resulting from an ignition of firedamp, ripped through the Old Coal Seam and claimed 45 lives. The 50th anniversary of the disaster was marked in 2010 with the unveiling of the 'Guardian', a 20m (66ft) tall statue, created by Sebastien Boyesen, which has inevitably become known as the Guardian of the Valleys – Wales's Angel of the North.

The rough grassland of the southern common has now given way to heather moorland and occasional bilberry, with meadow pipits and skylarks abundant and buzzards overhead. The track, very clear on the ground but surprisingly absent from the Explorer map, climbs just to the left of a double fence over the western shoulder of Waun Wen, with superb views over the Ebbw Fach Valley to Mynydd Carn-y-Cefn. The views get even better as the track rises to the west of the rounded summit of **Gwastad**, with the Bristol Channel gleaming both to the south-east and south-west, and the dissected plateau of the South Wales valleys to the west.

Continue on the track as it drops slightly to a col, with Cwmtillery reservoir briefly in view to the left and the deep gash of Nant Ffrwd to the right. The track continues remorselessly northward, climbing across grassland on the flank of Coety Mountain, with the peaks of the Brecon Beacons now providing a backdrop to views across the head of Cwm Tyleri.

An initially easy descent follows into the higher reaches of the valley, passing above **Blaentillery Farm**, close to the site of the Blaentillery drift mine, still in operation in the early 21st century. A stony track drops down steeply, becoming a lane that hugs the valley side above Cwmtillery reservoir. ▶

The reservoir was constructed in 1906 but fed, curiously, via aqueduct and tunnel from the Grwyne Fawr reservoir 18½ miles (30km) away in the Black Mountains.

Just beyond the reservoir, cut down on a streamside path to the main valley road and follow this past a further lake, now landscaped but once a feeder pond for the collieries further down the valley, to reach the village of **Cwmtillery**. The land here was described as 'rich and wooded' in the 18th century, but became a hive of mining activity in the 19th century, and it was only in 1982 that Cwmtillery colliery closed. A massive reclamation programme has since removed all but a few traces of the coal industry. ▶

The pit wheels still stand as a memorial to William Williams, who was killed in the Chartist uprising in Newport in 1839.

Take the road running along the east side of the valley to descend gently into **Abertillery**, a typical valleys town that has fallen on hard times with the end of heavy industry in the area. However, there is an attractive local museum depicting the history and heritage of the area, the second-oldest Victorian shopping arcade in Wales and, in St Michael's Church, a series of permanent works by local artist John Selway based on the Stations of the Cross.

WALK 18

The Raven Walk

Start/Finish	Cwmcarn visitor centre (ST 233 934)
Distance	12 miles (19km)
Ascent	920m (3020ft)
Time	6–8hrs
Map(s)	Explorer 152, 166
Public transport	Bus 151 runs every 10 minutes from Newport via Cwmcarn to Blackwood.

A terrific, well-signposted route in excellent walking country, this is nevertheless a tough walk that is not to be under-estimated, with three significant climbs from the valleys onto the ridge tops. The first is from Cwmcarn onto the flanks of Mynydd y Lan, heading for the isolated hilltop church at Mynyddislwyn. Then there is the ascent of Mynydd Machen, followed by a descent to cross the Ebbw River and a final climb to the charismatic summit of Twmbarlwm.

Beyond the car park at the impressive **Cwmcarn** visitor centre, the long-time base of a pioneering scenic drive and now also a mountain biking centre, take a path alongside the access road, eventually crossing it at a subway, rounding a playing field and climbing steps to reach the main road through the village. Just beyond the post office, turn left, follow the road to a subway and take Chapel Farm Terrace over the river and a railway bridge. Immediately turn left, then go straight ahead on a path that climbs to meet a forest road. Keep straight on here up a stony track and then across boggy terrain, until a stile gives access onto the Mynydd y Lan Common.

The change in scenery is dramatic: trees are replaced by bracken and heather and there is a tremendous view to the north. A path leads over stiles until, rounding a corner, the whitewashed church of **Mynyddislwyn**, once a possession of Llantarnam Abbey, appears ahead. Turn left along the road, passing the remains of the

motte-and-bailey castle at Twyn Tudur, and take the farm lane down to Cwm-cae-singrug. Just before the farm, veer left, then take a narrow path behind the house and drop down to cross the dam of the drained and disused Nant-y-draenog reservoir, built in 1894 but closed in 1979.

The medieval motte-and bailey at Twyn Tudur

Keep above the wooded valley on a level path that crosses a field to reach a lane. Turn left here, right down a farm road, left along another road and right at Ty Capel onto a narrow lane, which zigzags steeply down to the village of **Ynysddu**. Turn left by the Progressive Workingmen's Club, cross the main road and the Sirhowy River, pass the Ynysddu Hotel and take steps leading up on the left onto the trackbed of a dismantled railway. Follow this for half a mile (0.8km), and then take the path on the right leading up to the Ynys Hywel Activity Centre.

Behind the main building some rustic steps lead up to a path that passes a boarded-up camping barn and takes a level course high above the Sirhowy Valley. A short, sharp rise gains a forest road and the Sirhowy Valley Walk, which keeps the Raven Walk company for the next hour or so. Turn right at a waymark to follow a green path rising

129

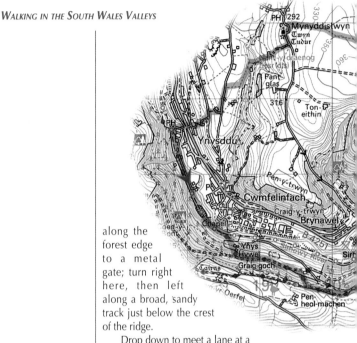

along the forest edge to a metal gate; turn right here, then left along a broad, sandy track just below the crest of the ridge.

Drop down to meet a lane at a cattle grid, but leave this immediately on the right. Climb a stony track and then go to the left of a metal barrier, seeking out the track that climbs to the crest of the ridge, now with the added bonus of a panoramic view to the south, across the Rhymney Valley to the wooded Craig Ruperra ridge and to the Severn Estuary beyond. The way ahead is straightforward, along a broad green track with the communications masts on Mynydd Machen straight ahead. ◄

An enormous waste tip on the right serves as a reminder that not every vestige of the valley's industrial past has been cleared.

A gentle slope leads up to the masts on the heathery summit of **Mynydd Machen**, with another 360-degree view, including the valleys of the Ebbw, Sirhowy and Rhymney and the intervening moorland. A broad green ride now descends the bracken-covered slopes to the east, with the Machen limestone quarry to the right. After 400m, the Raven Walk turns left, descending through bracken and then around the left-hand side of a huge field to

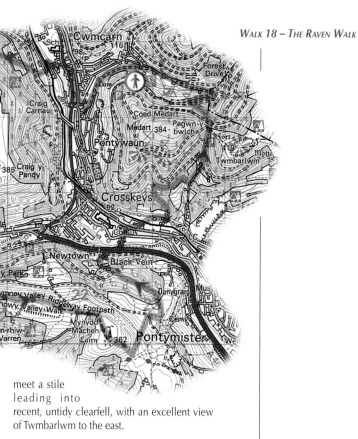

meet a stile
leading into
recent, untidy clearfell, with an excellent view
of Twmbarlwm to the east.

*Looking west along
the ridge from
Mynydd Machen*

Mynydd Machen from Pegwn-y-bwlch

The path improves and becomes a green woodland track, joining a surfaced lane at Glenside bungalow. Follow this as it drops below the by-pass, crosses the Ebbw River and reaches the main road in **Cross Keys**. Turn right, then left along Medart Street, which narrows to a footpath going over the railway and then climbs gently to reach the Crumlin arm of the Monmouthshire Canal. Quickly cross the canal on a bridge that provided the only access to Cwmbyr Farm. The track climbs steeply through woodland to a junction; turn right here, now with the scanty remains of the farm, abandoned when the surrounding slopes were afforested, down to the right.

The path improves, with forestry on the left and fields to the right, and Mynydd Machen is prominent across the Ebbw Valley. At the end of the last field, swing right, cross a small stream and take the path rising through bracken to reach a narrow lane. Turn left here, climbing steadily and leaving the lane to the right when the tarmac ends. Cross a forest road and climb on a green path to reach Pegwn-y-bwlch. Nearby, there is a wood-carving of a search-and-rescue dog and its handler.

At this point there is an option to take the unremittingly steep, irritatingly long path up to **Twmbarlwm**. For some this may be a climb too far at this stage of the walk, but the rewards are exceptional: the summit is defended by the ramparts of a huge Iron Age fort, there is a medieval castle mound on the eastern perimeter and the all-round panorama is unforgettable. ▶

Back at Pegwn-y-bwlch, take the waymarked path steeply downhill, with steps in places. Turn sharp right onto a wider track and then slant down on a path that reaches a tarmac road. Follow this to a lake close to the former coal washery and then back to the Cwmcarn visitor centre.

The view takes in the Severn Estuary and the Somerset coast, the hills above the Wye Valley and the dissected plateau of the valleys, with the distant peaks of the Brecon Beacons behind.

WALK 19
High Folly and packhorse trails

Start	Pontypool Park (SO 288 007)
Finish	Rising Sun Bridge, Abersychan (SO 270 042)
Distance	8 miles (13km)
Ascent	375m (1230ft)
Time	4–6hrs
Map(s)	Explorer 152, Outdoor Leisure 13
Public transport	Pontypool has a very frequent bus service from Newport. Abersychan has regular bus services to Pontypool and Newport. Bus X24 leaves Abersychan for Pontypool every 10 minutes.

This is, quite simply, one of the best walks in South Wales, and even better for being a little off the beaten track. It combines the most easterly ridge in the valleys, with easy walking and sumptuous views over the Usk Valley and the hills around Abergavenny, with an old trackway commandeered in late medieval times to export iron from Blaenavon before the arrival of the tramways.

Start at the leisure centre in **Pontypool Park**, climbing up to skirt to the right of the famous old rugby ground and then passing to the left of the dry ski slope. The setting

The Grotto in
Pontypool Park

Originally intended for family picnics and shooting parties, the Grotto is open only on summer weekends.

becomes much more rural as a well-marked trail leads up through wooded parkland to the Grotto, a squat little structure well guarded by railings, barbed wire and padlocks. It contains a vaulted ceiling, supported by six pillars decorated with shells, and its floor is made from animal teeth and bones. ◄

The scenery is already exceptional, with the Vale of Usk to the east, the Severn Estuary to the south and the hills beyond Pontypool to the south-west.

Beyond two kissing gates, the route converges with the first of the day's packhorse trails. This climbs steadily onto the ridge, with intermittent views of the Folly, a post-war replica of the original 18th-century tower. ◄

John Hanbury's 12m-high (39ft) tower was dismantled during World War II to prevent German bomber pilots using it as a navigation aid.

After crossing a track, the landscape becomes more open, with stonechats, redstarts, whitethroats and chiffchaffs all abundant. Just before **Coed Ithel**, the track drops down to cross a little valley and rise up a slightly sunken track to a heavy-duty steel gate, designed to prevent motorised access to the common land ahead.

The track broadens out to become an enjoyable green lane, crossing the broad whale-back of **Mynydd Garn-wen** Common. It is easy to drift too far left, into

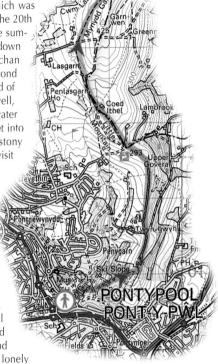

the enclosed fields above the isolated farmstead of Pen-y-ddoyga, which was burnt down and abandoned in the 20th century, but instead keep to the summit of the ridge before dipping down to cross the path from Abersychan to Penperlleni. To the right, beyond the delightfully named woodland of Coed Peggy Shams, is a holy well, Ffynnon Angaeron. The holy water comes from a stone structure set into the hillside and flows into a stony pool; occasionally, pilgrims still visit the site.

Head north from the pedestrian crossroads; the landscape is uneven here as a result of shallow quarrying, with the misshapen mountain of Skirrid Fawr suddenly rising into view ahead.

A long trek over the summit plateau of Mynydd Garnclochdy ensues, passing a telecoms mast on the left (a useful landmark later in the walk) and Garn-llech Farm on the right, and keeping straight on at another lonely junction of paths – the idiosyncratic Goose and Cuckoo pub (see walk 5) lies down to the right, but it may be regarded as a detour too far on this walk. The effort is minimal now, with a level green path picking its way between bilberries to the mountain road from **Cwmavon** to Llanover, which is followed to the left as far as a sharp right-hand bend at the site of Capel Newydd.

Map continues on page 137

Its site now marked only by an iron cross often festooned by wreaths, **Capel Newydd** was a non-conformist chapel built in the mid-18th century by two ladies from Blaenavon to serve the upper part of the

The site of Capel Newydd above Cwmavon

Pontypool Valley. The building was abandoned in 1860, but occasional open-air services are still held here.

Disregard the path leading into Blaenavon community woodland, and instead go back uphill for a few steps before turning onto the waymarked path heading south. This was a medieval packhorse trail, later used to carry 'pigs' of iron from Blaenavon to Newport. The trail is waterlogged in places (easy detours are available to avoid the worst spots) but, in general, forms a splendid green lane, taking a direct, level and very scenic course across the high moorland through heather, bracken and bilberry.

The trail heads just to the left of the prominent mast, the skyline now dominated by the surprisingly craggy western summit slopes of Mynydd Garnclochdy. As the woodland below comes to an end, the path passes a big crater on the left and joins a rough track that eventually becomes a narrow surfaced lane. It passes the curious sight of the disused Nant-y-Mailor reservoir, which was built by the

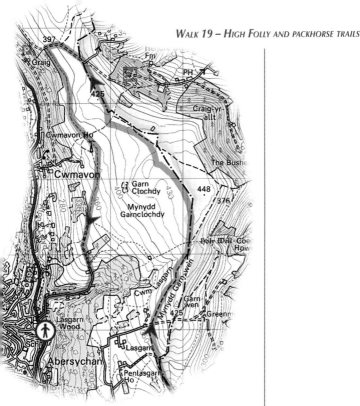

Pontypool Gas & Water Company in the 1890s and had a capacity of 4.5 million gallons, but is now eerily empty.

The lane drops down into the well-wooded Cwm Lasgarn, a peaceful backwater now but the site of a quarry opened in 1827 to supply limestone to the British Ironworks on the far side of the valley. ▶

Finally, cross the Afon Lwyd on Rising Sun Bridge and then pass over the line of the Blaenavon railway, now represented only by the name of a nearby house, the Old Halt, to reach the outskirts of **Abersychan**. Pontypool Park is only a couple of miles away, but there is no worthwhile footpath and a bus journey is recommended to complete a circular route.

The stone sleepers of the tramway which connected the quarry and the ironworks can still be discovered in the woods.

4 COAST AND VALE

The wave-cut platform and Blue Lias cliffs south of Trwyn y Witch (Walk 23)

WALK 20

The buried town of Kenfig

Start/Finish	Kenfig National Nature Reserve visitor centre (SS 802 810)
Distance	7 miles (11km)
Ascent	Negligible
Time	3–4hrs
Map(s)	Explorer 151, 165
Public transport	Bus 266 from Porthcawl to Pyle railway station (hourly services to Cardiff and Swansea) stops at the visitor centre six times a day.

This is a genuinely unique walk across the distinctive landscape of Kenfig and Margam Burrows, an extensive dune system, whose shifting sands overwhelmed 'Britain's Pompeii' – the prosperous borough of Kenfig – burying the church and houses and leaving just the remains of Kenfig Castle. The walk takes in the historic Prince of Wales Inn, the castle, the Cynffig Estuary, the broad beach of Kenfig Sands and the former Cistercian grange at Sker House.

Cross the road from the visitor centre and walk up Heol Ton, with bungalows to the left and open common on the right. After 200m, turn left into a narrow metalled lane, with horsiculture on one side and open views across arable fields and then pasture on the other. The lane runs behind Pool Farm, with the venerable Prince of Wales Inn soon in view ahead. ▶

Cross the main road again – there is a glimpse of Kenfig Pool, the focal point of a splendid nature reserve, through a gate – and head north along the pavement for 100m, then go left just before a bus stop onto a well-defined footpath. Take the right fork after 50m, savouring the wide view ahead over Kenfig Sands to Swansea Bay and the Gower hills. Follow the first two blue bridleway signs; it is easy to be seduced by these, but crucial not to follow the third sign. Instead, take the right-hand path below grassy dunes, heading almost due north. The going

The pub is well worth a visit: the wood-panelled upstairs room here, dating from the early 17th century, was once the Kenfig Corporation Guildhall.

The ruins of Kenfig Castle

is hard at times on a sandy path through dune slacks. Go through a gate and **Kenfig Castle** is in view ahead, easily reached across sandy heathland.

The lordship, castle, port and borough of **Kenfig** was established in the 12th century at a strategically important site where the Port Way (on the line of the Roman road from Cardiff to Neath) crossed the Cynffig Estuary. In the 14th century, Kenfig was a town of around 800 people, with St James's Church, a chapel and a hospital. By 1470, it had been virtually abandoned as the sand enveloped it. The antiquarian John Leland said in the 1530s that it was 'in ruins and almost shokid and devoured with the sandes that the Severne se there castith up'.

The scanty remains of the nearby healing well known as Ffynnon Legad ('bubbling spring') lie close to an abandoned meander loop of the **Afon Cynnfig**, which is then followed down to the coast. The attractive river mouth is well worth lingering over. Follow a broad grassy track known as the Old Haul Road, which runs behind the first line of grassed-over dunes. On the far side of the dunes the glorious sweep of golden **Kenfig Sands**, backed by a shingle bank, offers a very attractive low tide alternative.

The track behind the dunes becomes more gravelly as the low dark rocks of Sker Point come into view ahead. To the left is the remarkable expanse of low grassy dunes at the heart of the Kenfig National Nature Reserve and, further away, the hills behind Margam. On the right is the broad Severn Estuary, backed by the distant blue line of the Exmoor hills. At the foot of a slight rise, turn right to follow the top of the low cliffs round to Sker Point.

After savouring the views from the Point, retrace your steps as far as the fence marking the boundary of the nature reserve. Turn right just before this and pick up a track (ignore a coast path sign to the right). It passes in front of the imposing **Sker House**, a bulky rectangular house, which was recently rescued from dereliction. It was built on the site of a 12th-century grange farm, established by the Cistercians of Neath Abbey. ▶

One of the daughters of an 18th-century tenant farmer here inspired RD Blackmore (best known for Lorna Doone) to write The Maid of Sker, published in 1872.

Designated as a national nature reserve in 1989, **Kenfig National Nature Reserve** is one of the finest wildlife habitats in Britain. In summer, its dune

Kenfig Sands and Margam Mountain

slacks brim with orchids, including southern marsh orchid and the rare fen orchid. It is also the home of Kenfig Pool, the largest natural lake in South Wales, its reed beds home to water rail and wintering bittern and a wide array of wildfowl, and lightly grazed grasslands hosting an astonishing variety of insects, including the shrill carder bee.

The map shows a plethora of paths back to the visitor centre – but a direct route is impeded by barbed wire. It is altogether easier to go back to the point where the Sker Point route left the main track and then work inland from there, skirting the edge of the golf course, then trending left and following a wide path. The going is alternately easy on grass and trying on sand, until the visitor centre suddenly appears, only 90m or so ahead.

WALK 21

Ewenny Priory and Merthyr Mawr Warren

Start	Ewenny Priory (SS 912 778)
Finish	Newton church (SS 836 775)
Distance	9 miles (14km)
Ascent	220m (720ft)
Time	4–5hrs
Map(s)	Explorer 151
Public transport	Bus X2 from Cardiff via Bridgend to Porthcawl runs every half hour and stops close to both the start and finish of the walk.

This gentle but absorbing walk climbs onto the limestone downs above St Brides Major, crosses the River Ewenny on ancient stepping stones at Ogmore Castle and makes its way across the high dunes of Merthyr Mawr Warren. Highlights include the ruined priory at Ewenny, the Nant Baptismal Pool in Corntown, a clapper bridge (very rare in Wales) over the River Alun, Old Castle Down (rich in birds and butterflies in summer), and the substantial remains of Candleston Castle.

Sat virtually on the banks of the River Ewenny, the eponymous priory was founded as a Benedictine house in 1141 and became one of the best fortified ecclesiastical buildings in Britain, with a bulky curtain wall including six towers. The church is the most impressive Norman church in South Wales, with a magnificent presbytery. A footpath just east of the priory leads over a footbridge and stile into the little village of **Corntown**. Turn left and then look for the pond on the right, just before Heol-y-Cawl. ▸

Take Heol-y-Cawl as far as Corntown Farm, but on reaching the farm climb a stile on the right and zigzag across two fields to reach a minor road. Turn right here, then left before Tair Croes Farm onto a bridleway, which reaches a road junction at Wallas Fach. Turn left onto Wick Road, then right over a stile just beyond Wallas Farm. Angle left across the first field to find a stile, and then cut through the attractive woodland of Coed y

This is the Nant Baptismal Pool, once owned by Jesus College, Oxford, and later used by Bethlehem Baptist Chapel before it fell into disuse around 1900.

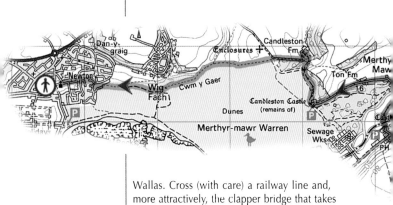

Wallas. Cross (with care) a railway line and, more attractively, the clapper bridge that takes the path over the River Alun on solid piers supporting stone slabs.

The route lies to the right along a narrow lane, with Coed y Bwl nature reserve on the left. This reserve, mainly consisting of ash woodland, has bluebells and wood anemones but is renowned for its sensational display of wild daffodils. ◄

The daffodils were planted in the early 19th century and more than 250,000 bloom each spring.

At the end of the wood, bear left up a steep track through the common land of Craig Ddu onto Old Castle Down. This classic heathland is one of the last refuges of the High Brown Fritillary butterfly in Wales. Once on the high ground, follow the fence around the edge of the open access land, swinging left to pass a solitary house, Brynawel, and then right to drop down to the northern outskirts of the village of **St Brides Major**. Go straight across the main road onto a surfaced lane, which leads up towards Ogmore Down, quickly becoming a green bridleway as it skirts Pant limestone quarry. The route here is on the line of Heol y Millwyr, said to be a Norman military road.

Take the green path running through gorse to cross Southerndown golf course and reach the road at **Ogmore**. A lane opposite leads down to Ogmore Castle, which is spectacularly sited on the banks of the Ewenny. Cross the river, either on the ancient stepping stones or, depending

on water levels or
the state of the tide,
on a bridge 400m
upstream, which
is accessed via
the main road.

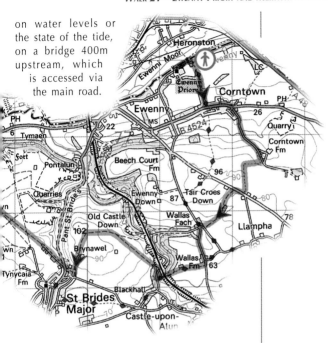

Beyond the
stepping stones a concreted path leads over the flat land
between the Ewenny and Ogmore rivers, before crossing the latter on a squat pedestrian suspension bridge.
On the far side, a lane leads quickly to the pretty village
of **Merthyr Mawr**, with its thatched cottages, tiny village
green and medieval church on an early Christian site.

> **Ogmore Castle** was built in 1116 by William de
> Londres. It was constructed of earth and timber,
> with a ditch that was filled with water on a tidal
> basis. It was reconstructed in stone, and the sur-
> viving keep is one of the oldest Norman structures
> in Wales. The castle was used as late as the 19th
> century as a court of justice, prison, and centre for
> collecting rents.

Candleston Castle

A lane running west from the village leads to Candleston Castle, situated on the edge of Merthyr Mawr Warren. The castle was really a small fortified manor house, built in the 14th century and occupied for 500 years; it is now a forlorn ivy-covered ruin. It was originally sited in the centre of the village of Treganlaw, which was buried, along with all its farmland, under sand dunes.

The most striking aspect of the **Merthyr Mawr Warren** dunes is their height – up to 80m (260ft), largely because the dunes lie on top of a limestone cliff. There is a rich assemblage of archaeological features beneath the dunes, including traces of Mesolithic man, Bronze Age cairns, Iron Age metalworking and a medieval settlement. In addition, there are shell middens, cultivation ridges and the remains of a 15th-century windmill on top of the dunes. Plants and wildlife include violets, orchids,

A thatched cottage at Merthyr Mawr

autumn gentian and fungi; cinnabar and six-spot burnet moths, a range of butterflies such as the brimstone and common blue; and wintering wildfowl.

Take the sandy track northwards from the castle towards Candleston Farm (an alternative bridleway passes close to the site of the windmill but is even harder going on soft, steep sand). Pass an old lime kiln and swing left to follow a track around the northern edge of the dunes. When the track swings right, go through the first of several kissing gates, then across soft sand on a path that undulates quite steeply across old dunes.

Beyond the hamlet of Wig-Fach, the path crosses Newton Burrows, shaded in part by coppiced hazel, and reaches **Newton** village along Puddle Lane. Aim to the right of the churchyard and past the Jolly Sailor pub to reach Newton church, a fortress church with look-out towers and a rich interior that boasts an unusual wall-mounted pulpit.

WALK 22

Castles around Cowbridge

Start/Finish	Cowbridge Town Hall (SS 996 746)
Distance	7 miles (11km)
Ascent	170m (560ft)
Time	3–4hrs
Map(s)	Explorer 151
Public transport	Bus X2 leaves Cardiff and Bridgend twice an hour and stops at Cowbridge.

The market town of Cowbridge is set in a largely agricultural landscape of low rolling hills and fertile valleys, interspersed with fascinating villages such as St Hilary, with its impressive stone and thatch buildings. But it is also a landscape of hillforts and castles, charting the evolution of defensive structures, from Iron Age enclosures through town walls and motte-and-bailey castles to fortified manor houses.

Leave Cowbridge along Eastgate, with its varied architectural styles. Number 44 was said to have been a medieval pilgrims' hospice and later an inn called the Ancient Druid. Next door is The Armoury, a well-preserved 18th-century town house on earlier foundations. Turn left at the traffic lights, with an old Turnpike Trust milestone at the junction, pass under the bypass and immediately take the footpath on the right that rises diagonally and quite steeply through woodland. Incline to the left at the top of the wood, following the same broad direction through three fields, with attractive views opening up of green hills to the west. A complicated double stile in wood and stone leads to a narrow lane, which runs down between tall hedges to the edge of **Aberthin**.

Turn left at the first road junction in the village, then right at the second, following the lane until, opposite the last house, a track heads up through the bracken, crossing the common land of Stalling Down. ◄

Stalling Down is also known as Bryn Owen, after the Welsh chieftain Owain Glyndwr, who is said to have defeated the forces of Henry IV in a battle on this hillside in 1405.

The hills to the west of Cowbridge

Away to the left, below a huge telecoms mast, is Llanquian Wood, with a substantial double-banked Iron Age hillfort concealed in deep undergrowth. The earth and rubble mounds of the Norman castle and chapel of Llanquian are a little closer to hand in the intervening valley.

The track keeps to the left of a delightful hilltop hay meadow, thick with wildflowers in summer, and then dips down to the left to skirt

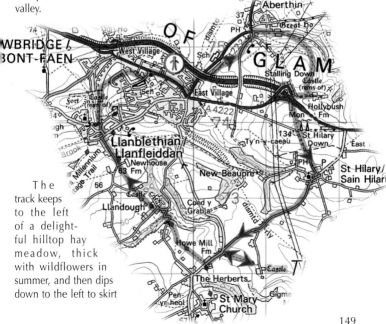

Hollybush Farm and reach a minor road near Downs Café. Follow this road over a dual carriageway and then take a lane on the left for 100m until, just beyond the unlikely sight of an Indian restaurant, there is a right turn onto a very pleasant green path that leads towards two more masts. Cross a track here, now with The Clump on the right. ◄

The way forward is now downhill on a wide track. The Severn Estuary and Devon hills are ahead, beyond the village of **St Hilary**, its church tower rising above a cluster of ancient cottages.

> **St Hilary** took its name from its church, the only one in Britain that is dedicated to St Hilarius, the fourth-century Bishop of Poitiers. St Hilary is a well-to-do village with a number of late medieval houses, several of them thatched, and a fine 17th-century inn, with an ancient interior. Opposite the inn, in the garden of Church Cottage, is a remarkable circular stone pigsty, which has a conical roof.

Take the country lane heading south-west as far as Howe Mill, a stone-built former corn mill, to see the remarkable Old Beaupre Castle, reached by a footpath that passes through the remains of water meadows, fishponds and formal gardens. ◄

Back at Howe Mill, take the road for a further 200m, then go over a stile and through three large fields to reach a lane dropping down to Castle Precinct at **Llandough**. Just to the right is another former mill, in use until the 1920s, while The Cottage was once the rectory, with a curious stone-built adjunct, which once housed a beehive.

Go left at a road junction, then right along a lane to view the remains of Llandough Castle, another fortified manor house with a 15th-century turret, three-storey gatehouse and walls of various dates including the scanty remains of a late medieval tower house. Return to the road and pick up a path going north-west past Newhouse Farm to reach the substantial village of

This circular plantation was known as the Hanging Wood because convicts were marched up from Cowbridge to be executed here.

Actually a fortified manor house rather than a castle, Old Beaupre has a gatehouse dating from 1585 and a remarkable Renaissance porch, constructed 15 years later.

The Renaissance porch at Old Beaupre

Llanblethian, and more evidence of the troubled past of this area. Up to the left is Caer Dynnaf, a multivallate hillfort that housed a number of farmsteads, while across the valley is the impressive 12th-century keep of St Quintin's Castle, enlarged in the 14th century in a style reminiscent of Caerphilly Castle and later used as a prison.

The route through Llanblethian passes a woollen factory, which housed two looms in a former water mill, before taking a footpath at the base of the river cliff to enter **Cowbridge** along The Butts, with the 14th century town walls on the left. Beyond the walls is the Physic Garden, dedicated to exhibiting the curative properties of plants, while the remaining town gate and the 17th-century grammar school are just to the right, close to the impressive parish church, which lies close to High Street and the town hall with its clock tower and bellcote.

151

WALK 23

The Glamorgan Heritage Coast

Start	Ogmore-by-Sea car park (SS 861 755)
Finish	Llantwit Major church (SS 965 686)
Distance	10 miles (16km)
Ascent	390m (1280ft)
Time	4–6hrs
Map(s)	Explorer 151
Public transport	Bus 145 runs hourly between Bridgend and Llantwit Major, calling at Ogmore-by-Sea.

This is a deceptively strenuous walk along an impressive stretch of coastline. It uses part of the Glamorgan Heritage Coast path and the tremendously ambitious all-Wales coastal path, the completion of which has opened up the last remaining 'hidden' bits of the Heritage Coast. Highlights include the dramatic crumbling cliffs, the spectacular beaches at Dunraven Bay and Traeth Mawr, and the striking lighthouses at Nash Point.

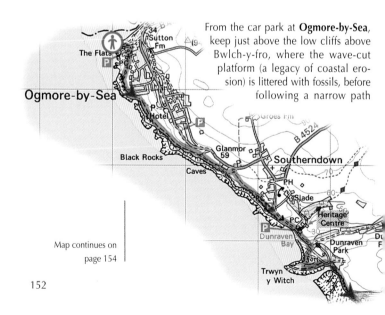

From the car park at **Ogmore-by-Sea**, keep just above the low cliffs above Bwlch-y-fro, where the wave-cut platform (a legacy of coastal erosion) is littered with fossils, before following a narrow path

Map continues on page 154

upwards as the cliffs get steeper. The views ahead to the golden sands of Dunraven Bay are gorgeous, while Porthcawl and the Ogmore Estuary can be seen behind. Cross a steeply incised dry valley and stride out across the closely cropped turf to reach a wall guarding the Dunraven Valley. The green path to the right of the access road heads straight down to the car park and information centre.

Once through the gates that provide access to the **Dunraven Park** estate, keep to the right on the high ground around the prominent headland of Trwyn y Witch. The reward is sensational scenery, as the path drops down through woodland, with frequent glimpses of the sands, wave-cut platforms and dramatic Blue Lias cliffs leading south-eastwards along the Heritage Coast.

The imposing early 19th-century mansion on the site of **Dunraven Castle** was inhabited until the 1940s, but the crumbling ruins were finally demolished in 1963. The original castle was constructed in the 12th century, and the surviving walled garden and castellated ice house date from the 16th century

The superb beach at Dunraven Bay

Beyond an information board, the path continues along the clifftop before negotiating Cwm-Mawr, a deep, wooded hanging valley, whose stream reaches the beach via a small waterfall. The clifftop path now runs above the wide sandy expanse of **Traeth Bach**, with a remarkable aerial view of a large stack of Blue Lias limestone, which has slipped away from the cliff and is now poised precariously above the beach. A steep descent leads into Cwm Bach, a second hanging valley, providing access to the beach of Traeth Bach, but only by way of two steel ladders, which make up an unusual and challenging via ferrata.

The path leads back to the remarkably level clifftop plateau, a remnant of the Pliocene marine platform, 60m (197ft) above sea level, where swallows can be seen skimming above the fields to pick up insects. The route leads easily across the stone-walled fields above the even larger golden beach of Traeth Mawr, its abrupt cliffs providing secure nesting places for peregrine falcons. Kestrels, which are

Map continues on page 156

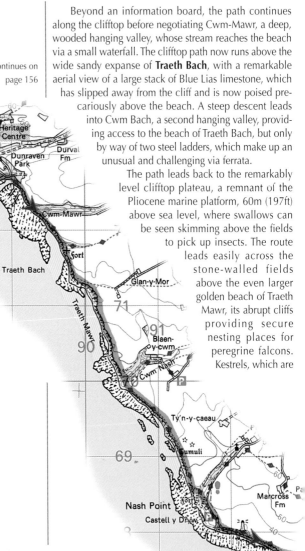

154

sadly in decline elsewhere, and buzzards are also often seen along this stretch of the coast.

Access along the clifftop to Cwm Nash, where another stream dissects the clifftop plateau, is informal but permitted by the landowner. There is a steep descent and an equally steep climb out of the valley, while an easy stroll inland up the valley reaches the hamlet of **Monknash**, the site of a former grange farm of Neath Abbey and an outstanding historic pub, the Plough and Harrow. Back on the coast, it is worth keeping away from the edge of the cliffs east of Cwm Nash: the profile of the cliffs has changed over the years, and there are more blocks ready to tumble.

The path heads south-east across arable fields, with the two lighthouses at **Nash Point** now visible ahead. Drop down into Cwm Marcross through scrubby woodland, which partially conceals the ramparts of an Iron Age hillfort, and cross the over-deepened valley, which was scoured out by meltwater at the end of the last Ice Age. An easy path leads up to a little café; head right here, on a green path that hugs the clifftop, before going to the

The lighthouses at Nash Point

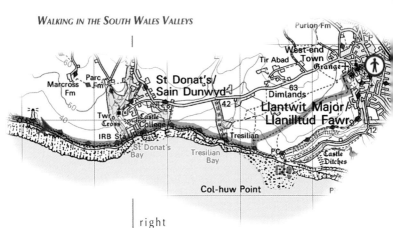

right
of the two
lighthouses. These
were constructed in response to the outcry that followed
the sinking of the passenger steamer *Frolic* in 1830. ◄

These were the last manned lighthouses in Wales and were automated in 1998; conducted tours are provided by Trinity House.

Beyond a stone stile, it is worth pausing to savour the view back to the lighthouses above the serrated cliffs, which are composed of thin layers of Jurassic limestones and mudstones, deeply faulted and jointed and pockmarked with caves. At the top of the cliffs, the vegetation is sculpted by the prevailing south-westerly wind into curiously asymmetrical shapes. These cliffs also represent the eastern limit of the territory reclaimed by the chough, an iconic bird of closely cropped cliff top grasslands. The path passes through a series of big fields with stone walls, now with the striking cliffs of the island of Steep Holm to the right, and the summits of the Quantock Hills very prominent on the far side of the Severn Estuary.

Beyond another stile, the way ahead lies between a bramble hedge to the right and a post-and-wire fence protecting a huge arable field to the left. A level path then leads through woodland – providing welcome shade on summer days – before dropping steeply down a flight of steps to emerge, wholly unexpectedly, by the slipway running down from **St Donat's Castle**. The castle was built in the 12th century and since 1962 has been home to Atlantic College, a renowned international school.

At the far side of the little bay the path rises through scrubby woodland, reaches the open clifftop briefly, with an enticing prospect of more cliffs, caves and bays running eastward, and then reaches King George's Field, with easy, level walking on springy turf. Stone steps lead down to the cluster of whitewashed houses at Tresilian Bay, where there is no alternative to clambering across the impressive storm beach. Beyond the bay the path rises again – there is an excellent retrospective view of the huge Reynard's Cave on the western side of the bay – passes a pillbox and descends to the Dimhole, a miniature dry valley.

Follow the path inland to a stile and turn right to follow the right-hand edge of an enormous field, often sown with oilseed rape – a surprisingly good crop for birds such as yellowhammer. At the field boundary, keep straight on, now on Church Lane, a straight green track between bramble hedges. The lane becomes stony and descends gently, with **Llantwit Major** now in view ahead. Bear left at a junction of tracks to pass a dovecote and the 14th-century gatehouse that controlled entry to the Tewkesbury Abbey estate. Now take a stepped path down to St Illtyd's Church, founded around AD500 and an important seat of learning for the early Welsh saints, with an important collection of Celtic crosses and carved stones. Beyond the church is the historic centre of Llantwit, with a cluster of ancient buildings, none more impressive than the Norman manorial courthouse, which later became a guildhall.

WALK 24
The Border Vale

Start/Finish	Ystradowen church (ST 011 776)
Distance	9 miles (14km)
Ascent	210m (690ft)
Time	4–6hrs
Map(s)	Explorer 151
Public transport	Bus E11 makes eight journeys a day between Cowbridge and Talbot Green, passing Ystradowen church and also Pontyclun railway station (hourly services to Cardiff and Bridgend).

This is a gentle walk in the northern Vale of Glamorgan. It travels through grassland and woods, past the unfinished motte-and-bailey castle at Ystradowen, the Talygarn estate – with its chapel of ease, impressive house and parkland featuring exotic trees and an exquisite lake – the heronry, gentry farmhouse and model farm at Llwyn Rhyddid, and Castell Tal-y-fan, an important Norman castle now reduced to fragmentary remains.

This is an abandoned motte (the only unfinished castle mound in Wales), built on the end of a glacial moraine.

Go through the kissing gate by the side of St Owain's Church in **Ystradowen**, which has a wooded mound to the left. ◀ Head for a stile at the far edge of the field. From here it is tempting to follow a level path that passes a little pond, but the true route lies much higher, passing just below **Ash Hall**, the largest house in the parish, which once boasted kitchen, water and rose gardens. Aim for a stile by a clump of trees, and negotiate a small field and a gravelled drive to arrive at a minor road. The Millennium Heritage Trail comes in from the left here and is followed all the way to Llwyn Rhyddid.

The route lies through the gate opposite Ash Cottage and straight across a field. Here, the character of the landscape changes, with easy walking over attractive limestone downs, and wide views to the hills of Bro Morgannwg. The path, still with Millennium Trail waymarks, snakes through a patch of conifer woodland. Turn left along a narrow road between hazel hedges,

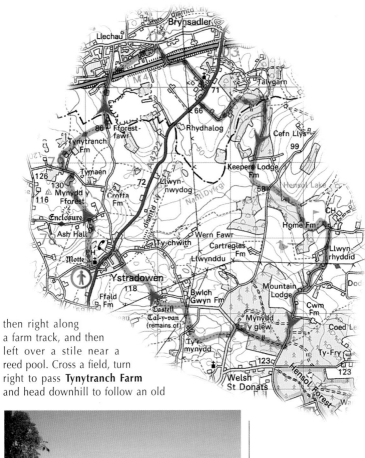

then right along
a farm track, and then
left over a stile near a
reed pool. Cross a field, turn
right to pass **Tynytranch Farm**
and head downhill to follow an old

The view north
to Mynydd
Garthmaelwg from
east of Tynytranch
Farm

159

boundary between arable fields. At a country lane, turn left, passing under trees.

Somewhat surprisingly, the road becomes suburban and then passes over the M4. Immediately turn right, along a well-defined path that eventually threads its way between new housing (ignore a gate on the right) to reach an abandoned road. Turn right along this, right again at the main road, and right again at The Elms, an old farmhouse, to take a track back over the M4 and into quieter territory, heading for **Talygarn**. The forlorn ivy-covered remains of the old chapel of ease of St Anne's Church lie beyond its 19th-century replacement to the side of the track, which now swings right through housing to reach the main road. Turn right here, then left under chestnut trees along a private drive to Cot Farm. Beyond the farm, a quite delightful track drops down through woodland to reach the parkland surrounding Talygarn House, with the house and then the lake glimpsed through trees.

> There has been a house on the **Talygarn estate** since the 14th century. Although it was transformed into a Tudor Gothic mansion in the 1870s, its principal rooms were lavishly decorated in a rich Italianate style. Having spent much of the 20th century as a convalescent home for miners and then an NHS physiotherapy clinic, it is now once again in private hands. The grounds retain their former splendour, with sloping lawns, exotic trees and shrubs, and a beautiful tree-fringed lake.

The track swings right at the foot of the lake, now seen at its best, before heading slightly uphill to pass Keepers Lodge Farm, with views of the boggy moorland known as Morfa Ystradowen away to the west. Keep straight ahead here, crossing two fields to reach a narrow lane. Turn left, then right after only 70m on a path through conifer woodland. Head half-right across a field, climb a stile beside a gate, and then drop down across a second field with woodland and then a very attractive small lake, Llwyn-yoy Pond, to the right.

Llwyn-yoy Pond

Follow the lake round to the right, now with the Vale of Glamorgan Hotel's golf course to the left; the track is initially separated from the fairway by a belt of young trees, but then heads over a stile into woodland. To the right is the Coed Llwyn Rhyddid nature reserve, home to one of the largest heronries in Wales, with around 28 pairs of herons recorded in recent years. ▶

The sometimes damp track skirts Home Farm to reach a minor road. Turn right here, passing an array of somewhat dilapidated barns, with the golf course still to the left. Surprisingly, there is no view of the early 19th-century gentry farmhouse and adjacent model farm of **Llwyn-rhyddid** from the road – take a boggy path on the right for 100m to gain one – and the mill pond is disappointingly hidden behind a dense thicket of trees. Press on to the road at Mountain Lodge and follow it into **Hensol Forest**, which dates back to at least 1600.

Turn right onto a broad forest ride, keeping to the dead-straight track as it makes its way easily through the trees. Recent restoration has removed non-native trees and let more light into the woodlands. Go left onto a road at the car park, and right after only 150m onto a

Nesting herons have been recorded in the Hensol area since 1872, and can be seen from the road north of Llwyn Rhyddid during the breeding season, from mid-January until August.

clear footpath heading for Ty'r Mynydd; from here a good path rises over open pasture to a road. Bear left here, and then veer right through a gate to reach **Castell Tal-y-fan**. It is hard to pick out the remains, but there are tantalising glimpses of one of the vale's most romantic ruins.

> A grand medieval castle established in the 12th century and once the centre of a lordship extending over seven parishes, **Castell Tal-y-fan** is now reduced to scanty remains cloaked in woodland. The castle had a high curtain wall with towers and an impressive gateway, but lay in ruins by the 16th century. A farmhouse, also now ruined, was built onto the castle around 1700. What remains is a fragment of a great round tower, parts of the curtain wall and, in the farmhouse, a bread oven that was used in living memory.

Beyond the castle ruins, go through a gate and turn left, then quickly right onto a field path that crosses the long-disused Pontyclun to Cowbridge railway, opened in 1865 and axed by Beeching 99 years later. The path reaches the Badger's Brook estate and the village of Ystradowen.

WALK 25

Deserted villages and folk museum

Start	Cosmeston Lakes Country Park (ST 177 691)
Finish	St Fagans (ST 121 771)
Distance	9 miles (14km)
Ascent	330m (1080ft)
Time	4–6hrs
Map(s)	Explorer 151
Public transport	Bus 94 runs twice an hour between Cardiff and Barry via Penarth and Cosmeston; buses 32, 320 and 322 provide at least an hourly service between St Fagans and Cardiff.

This walk runs close to Cardiff but is full of surprises, from Cosmeston Lakes Country Park, with its reconstructed medieval village, to the outstanding open-air National History Museum at St Fagans, renowned for its remarkable collection of relocated buildings. On the way, the walk passes the glacial meltwater gorge at Cwm George, the attractive pools known as the Salmon Leaps at Michaelston-le-Pit, and the landscaped park and Regency villa at Coedaryhdyglyn.

Follow the boardwalk from the **Cosmeston** visitor centre to the medieval village, and then take the concrete track that skirts the village to reach the Mile Road. The village dates from the 12th century but the manor house was already in ruins by 1437. ▶

The Mile Road is an

Archaeologists have been patiently uncovering the evidence for the village since the 1970s, and in parallel a 'medieval' village has been reconstructed on the site.

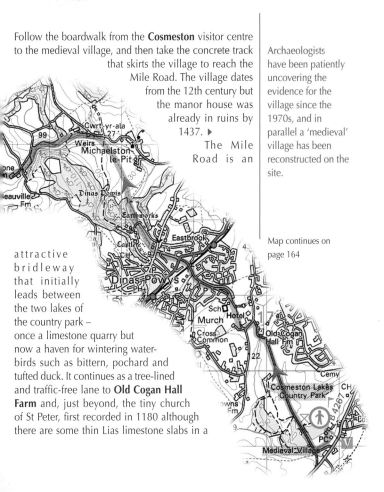

Map continues on page 164

attractive bridleway that initially leads between the two lakes of the country park – once a limestone quarry but now a haven for wintering water-birds such as bittern, pochard and tufted duck. It continues as a tree-lined and traffic-free lane to **Old Cogan Hall Farm** and, just beyond, the tiny church of St Peter, first recorded in 1180 although there are some thin Lias limestone slabs in a typically Saxon brickwork pattern. Old Cogan is another deserted medieval village, and there are house platforms, the site of a mill and a long water leat in the fields around the church.

At the end of the Mile Road, turn left along a country road, then quickly right and right again into a sunken lane, now closed to traffic. Follow suburban roads down to traffic lights close to the centre of the suburban village of **Dinas Powys** and continue ahead along Millbrook Road. Go straight across at the next road junction onto a track that quickly becomes a narrow path hemmed in between a brook (the crumbling remains of the keep and curtain wall of Dinas Powys Castle are up to the left) and a large field.

Immediately after negotiating two stiles, turn left onto a track that leads into Cwm George, an attractively wooded limestone gorge, which was a glacial meltwater channel at the end of the last Ice Age. Up to the right is another early medieval castle on the site of an Iron Age promontory fort. A good and popular path leads between fields down to the Cadoxton River on the outskirts of **Michaelston-le-Pit**.

Turn left along the road, pass the lowest of several pools and go through a kissing gate on the left. The path leads over a stile to the upper pools, home to mallard, moorhen, little grebe and heron. The picturesque complex of dams, weirs and pools is known as the Salmon Leaps, and an easy path leads alongside them and into a delightful wood, with ferns, bluebells, the scent of wild garlic and the fluttering of woodland butterflies.

Keep to the path as it rises and crosses a field to reach Wrinstone Farm. Go diagonally right across three fields, cross a disused railway and follow the signposts to reach and (using a footbridge) cross a busy road on the way into **Wenvoe**. Keep straight on then turn right into Wallston Road; at the end go straight ahead to reach the Upper Orchid Field. ▶

Managed as a traditional meadow, the field has wildflowers such as primroses and cowslips in spring and is awash with orchids in June.

Turn left on encountering a road, then quickly right into Twyn yr Odyn, heading past a TV mast on a

St Fagans Castle

165

magnificent green path and crossing open access land to reach **The Downs**.

Turn left along a lane that approaches the busy A48. Cross this carefully and take the path across a field to a stone stile; angle left here to pass Old Coedarhydyglyn and cross a huge field to a stile in the far corner. Another stile leads into woodland, with a well-defined path winding downhill between bluebell woods and an arboretum. Negotiate a stile to reach a junction of paths; a detour to the right here gives glimpses of Coedarhydyglyn itself. ◀

Back at the junction of paths take the left-hand option, over stiles and through gates on the way to the Greendown Inn, close to the heavily restored St George's-super-Ely church. Go past the pub, but before reaching the church turn right onto a path that leads to an unusual and interesting footbridge crossing the River Ely, and that simultaneously passes beneath the main South Wales railway line. The path then leads under a dual carriageway and up to and alongside the access road leading to the National History Museum (no admission charge) at **St Fagans**.

> Surrounded by an intact picturesque landscaped park, Edwardian wooded dell and walled kitchen garden, Coedarhydyglyn is a neo-classical Regency villa, built in 1820 to replace an older house.

> One of the best open-air museums in Europe and set in parkland surrounding the Elizabethan manor house of St Fagans Castle, the **National History Museum** is both an outstanding tourist attraction and a valuable educational resource. The centrepiece is the collection of 40 buildings that have been re-erected here, including farmhouses, a toll-house, a cockpit, a workman's institute, a Celtic village, a row of ironworkers' houses, a school and a chapel. Most remarkably of all, St Teilo's Church was moved stone by stone to the museum and is decorated as it would have been in the past, with superb murals and paintings.

5 HISTORY AND HERITAGE

Innovative public art on the Trevithick Trail (Walk 28)

WALK 26
St Illtyd's Walk in upland Gower

Start	Pontarddulais (SN 592 037)
Finish	Pontardawe (SN 727 046)
Distance	14½ miles (23km)
Ascent	540m (1770ft)
Time	6–8hrs
Map(s)	Explorer 165 (very small sections of the route are covered by Explorer 178 and Outdoor Leisure 12)
Public transport	Bus X13 runs twice an hour between Swansea and Pontarddulais (there is also a very infrequent train service); buses X20, X25 and 120 provide a similar level of service between Pontardawe and Swansea.

This excerpt from the 64-mile (103km) St Illtyd's Way is a long, satisfying tramp over the hills of upland Gower, with great views to the Preseli Hills and the Black Mountain. The route encounters several burial chambers, medieval house platforms, the striking earthen ramparts of Penlle'r Castell, and the isolated chapels at Gerazim and Baran, now in only occasional use.

> **St Illtyd** was at his most influential at the turn of the sixth century, when he was abbot of the important monastery at Llanilltyd Fawr (Llantwit Major). He is credited with improving farming practices in Wales and helping the Welsh to reclaim land from the sea. He is also more fancifully said to have relieved famine in Brittany. The walk runs between two churches named after him, in Pembrey (Carmarthenshire) and Neath.

From the Loughor Bridge in **Pontarddulais**, the route lies along Water Street, passing the stone that commemorates the attack on the town gate during the Rebecca Riots in 1843, and then along Dulais Road, Glynhir Road, Caecerrig Road and Dantwyn Road. Eventually, it turns left at a St Illtyd's Walk waymark onto a tarmac track

(Heol Ddwr) and climbs up past an oddly suburban cluster of houses to reach the open, bracken-covered common land of Graig Fawr.

The ruined farmhouse of Llandremor-uchaf lies down to the right, beyond the upright stones of a Neolithic burial chamber near Garreg Lwyd. ▸

The route now aims for the summit of Graig Fawr, climbing on a pleasant green track past the remains of medieval house platforms (probably summer dwellings for shepherds) up to a trig point surrounded by the severely eroded remains of an Iron Age fort. A little further along the broad ridge, beyond a slight depression, is the true summit of Graig Fawr, with an outstanding view westwards to the Preseli Mountains in Pembrokeshire.

St Illtyd's Walk now drops down to the col at the head of **Cwmcerdinen**, passing close to the lonely, gaunt Gerazim Chapel, built in 1811 and now very sparingly used, and to Blaen-gerdinen Farm. Beyond the col, an easy climb over the rounded hill of Pentwyn Mawr provides exhilarating walking on springy turf. The way lies above two conifer plantations to the mountain road between Swansea and Ammanford. The official route of the walk follows the road to the left, but ignore this. Instead, take the thin, damp track straight ahead. Very

This farmhouse was the first Methodist place of worship in the area, established in 1740 when the farmer, John Morgan, experienced an instant conversion on hearing the preacher Hywel Harries.

Map continues on page 170

169

quickly the earthen ramparts of **Penlle'r Castell** can be seen on the left.

Penlle'r Castell stands at the highest point of upland Gower and was constructed in the 13th century as a defensive stronghold designed to protect a remote and vulnerable frontier. Little remains of the crude masonry fortifications, but the surviving earthworks, with a deep ditch surrounding an inner bailey, are hugely impressive in their wild moorland setting, with sensational all-round views, including Swansea Bay

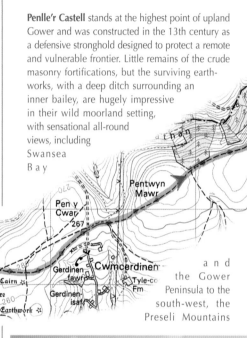

and the Gower Peninsula to the south-west, the Preseli Mountains

The impressive ramparts of Penlle'r Castell

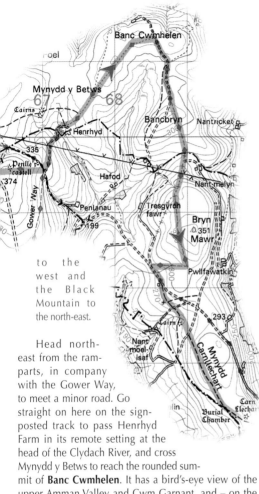

Map continues on page 172

to the west and the Black Mountain to the north-east.

Head north-east from the ramparts, in company with the Gower Way, to meet a minor road. Go straight on here on the sign-posted track to pass Henrhyd Farm in its remote setting at the head of the Clydach River, and cross Mynydd y Betws to reach the rounded summit of **Banc Cwmhelen**. It has a bird's-eye view of the upper Amman Valley and Cwm Garnant, and – on the far side of the valley, beyond Gwaun-Cae-Gerwen – the unlikely sight of a trotting track.

Follow the bridleway south from Banc Cwmhelen, across the flanks of Bancbryn, down to the Nant Melyn and then to the west of the rounded summit of Banc Mawr. Eventually, turn left along a minor road with the attractive but remote Baran Chapel in the middle of the

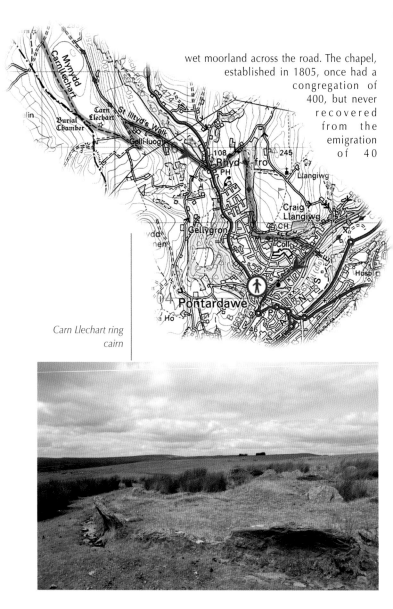

wet moorland across the road. The chapel, established in 1805, once had a congregation of 400, but never recovered from the emigration of 40

Carn Llechart ring cairn

local families to Pennsylvania at the end of the 19th century.

It is well worth diverting again here from the official walk, which follows the minor road south-east towards Pontardawe. A better alternative is to follow the track across **Mynydd Carnllechart** (keeping just below the summit of the ridge), to reach the best of several Bronze Age ring cairns in the area. ▶

An earlier Neolithic chambered tomb, with a substantial capstone, lies just to the south-west of the ring cairn.

Continue south-eastwards from Carn Llechart to link up with a track heading above Gelli-luog-uchaf. Follow this around a hairpin bend and back down to the Baran Road (avoid at all costs a path on the right, which promises a shortcut but leads into an impassable mire). Follow the road downhill to the A474 at **Rhyd-y-Fro**, cross the main road, and take the minor lane opposite as far as Gwrhyd Cottages, before turning right onto a footpath that skirts a golf course and eventually reaches the B4603 on the northern outskirts of **Pontardawe**. Turn right here to reach the town centre and the end of an inspiring walk.

Carn Llechart is particularly striking when approached from this direction; its 25 stone slabs – all of which protrude outwards – surround a ruined burial chamber.

WALK 27
Sarn Helen

Start	Banwen (SN 855 096)
Finish	Aberdulais (SS 772 993)
Distance	9 miles (14km)
Ascent	250m (820ft)
Time	4–6hrs
Map(s)	Outdoor Leisure 12, Explorer 166 (small section of route), Explorer 165
Public transport	Bus 158 provides an hourly service from Swansea via Neath and Aberdulais Falls to Banwen.

This is a fine ridge walk following the line of the Roman road from close to the Roman auxiliary fort at Coelbren across Hirfynydd (the 'long mountain') towards the rather more important fort at Neath. Climbing past Banwen, the route reaches the square fortlet on Hirfynydd and crosses the tussocky moorland of Penybegwyn, then drops down to the National Trust-owned Aberdulais Falls, with substantial remains of water turbines and a tinplate works.

Excavations in the 1990s revealed that the Roman road here consisted of cobbles laid directly on the underlying surface, with a drainage ditch cut into the clay.

Take the road through **Banwen**, passing through a landscape ravaged by copper, iron ore, tin and coal mining, but now largely restored. The site of the demolished Pantyddrainen Hotel and then the Kingdom Hall are on the right. ◀

At the end of the village, keep straight on, along a track that is prohibited to vehicles except in high summer. The track is at first concreted but soon becomes unsurfaced as it swings left (a tempting but steep short-cut goes off to the right here) and reaches a junction at a notice warning that the area ahead is both a motor sports arena and a windfarm construction site!

To the left, the ground drops away beyond Banwen to Coelbren, the site of an auxiliary fort on Sarn Helen. The fort survives as a massive rectangular enclosure, its defending rampart constructed from alternating layers of clay, turf and brushwood; an even larger marching camp nearby is just discernible.

However, the route lies to the right, along what is now a wide access road. Follow it uphill as it curves left, and at the next junction go straight on (using a forest road signposted as the Vale of Neath

Map continues on page 176

Walk), now mercifully away from the windfarm access route. The view can now be savoured, with a stunning panorama of the Brecon Beacons to the north, from the Carmarthen Fan through Fforest Fawr to Pen-y-fan.

One of the best preserved Roman roads in Wales, **Sarn Helen** ran from Neath to Y Gaer near Brecon, via the auxiliary fort at Coelbren. For much of its course it was a traditionally straight road, although as it climbed up to and descended from the Hirfynydd ridge it was forced to take a less direct route. The sites of Roman fortlets can still be discerned on the ridge, and the agger or embankment and its ditches survive in a number of places.

At the next junction, the way forward is quite clear, past the Gnoll Stones – with a replica of a ninth-century carving – and onto a much narrower, waymarked stony

The Hirfynydd Slab at the Gnoll Stones

175

track. There is a steady climb onto the Hirfynydd ridge, on a track that is worn to the bedrock in places, yet in others is grassy and sometimes rutted. The forest is set back some way on the right, allowing the mountain panorama to be savoured. Once the long summit ridge is reached, the conditions underfoot become quite trying in places, with deep ruts and considerable waterlogging as a result of off-road vehicle use that is clearly inappropriate on this historic route.

Forest is replaced by open grassland on the right, and a stile near a stone waymark leads over the fence to the

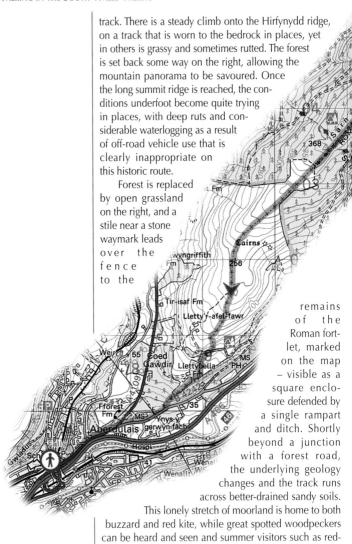

remains of the Roman fortlet, marked on the map – visible as a square enclosure defended by a single rampart and ditch. Shortly beyond a junction with a forest road, the underlying geology changes and the track runs across better-drained sandy soils. This lonely stretch of moorland is home to both buzzard and red kite, while great spotted woodpeckers can be heard and seen and summer visitors such as redstarts are abundant.

The level track, stony in places, passes a quarry close to a fire tower and then a curious representation of a Roman centurion's face before running across a relatively open area, where heather, bilberries and brambles replace the trees. The view suddenly opens out on the left, across the wooded slopes of the Neath Valley. Up to the right is a trig point on the edge of a burial chamber that crowns the small hill of Penybegwyn.

Sarn Helen continues straight ahead, crossing the footpath followed by St Illtyd's Walk, before losing height quite suddenly and reaching a gate marking the end of the forest. Beyond the gate lies the common land of Waun Glyn-nyd, with a rutted green lane now following the course of the Roman road. The way lies through gorse, bilberry and heather, with two cairnfields concealed in the vegetation. ▶

The Roman road leaves the common through a gate and continues as a pleasant green track, with traces of the agger and ditch in places, before passing the abandoned farmstead of Lletty'r-afel-fach. Keep straight on at two

Around 20 cairns are clustered in two groups; it is uncertain whether they had a religious significance or were simply by-products of agricultural clearance.

The Hirfynydd ridge from Glan-rhyd

177

The Tennant Canal aqueduct at Aberdulais

intersections with local footpaths and curve down on a rather muddier track through sparse woodland. The route swings right to follow a stony lane, still on the line of Sarn Helen, but there is then a sharp left turn to reach the modern road, which runs alongside the cricket ground at Ynys-y-gerwyn and joins the A4109 (thankfully with a pavement alongside) to reach **Aberdulais Falls**.

> The dramatic **Aberdulais Falls** have provided power for industry since 1584, when their energy was harnessed for copper production. Later, there was a corn mill at the site, and, later still, a tinplate works, with extensive remains still visible today. Above the waterfalls, the wooded gorge, with its nature trails, is worth exploring, while the restored waterwheel is the largest in use in Europe for electricity generation.

Immediately across the main road is a final sight not to be missed – the low viaduct carrying the Tennant Canal across the River Neath. The 10-arched masonry viaduct, with a cast-iron trough over an earlier navigable channel immediately to the north, was built in 1823 and is the longest canal aqueduct in South Wales. It is a fitting end to an historic walk.

WALK 28
The Trevithick Trail

Start	Penydarren Road, Merthyr Tydfil (SO 051 066)
Finish	Navigation House, Abercynon (ST 084 948)
Distance	9½ miles (15km)
Ascent	Negligible
Time	4–5hrs
Map(s)	Explorer 166
Public transport	There is a half-hourly train service between Cardiff and Merthyr, via Abercynon.

This is a journey in the steps of industrial history, tracing the route of the Merthyr tramroad, which on 21 January 1804 saw Richard Trevithick's Penydarren become the first steam-powered locomotive in the world to travel pulling a load – in this case 10 tonnes of iron. The walk includes Trevithick's Tunnel, the oldest railway tunnel in the world, together with substantial evidence of the area's industrial heritage, including the old stone sleeper blocks of the tramway itself.

The trail starts from the monument commemorating the epic journey, at the southern extremity of Samuel Homfray's Penydarren Ironworks, with the faded Theatre Royal alongside. Turn left, then immediately right into Tramroadside North. Its name and that of Tramroad Terrace are immediate indications of the historic associations of the route. Go past the disused town hall and the sad wreck of the Miners' Hall, skirting the town centre. Just above a roundabout, take a back lane known as Tramroadside South. A waymark after 300m provides welcome evidence that this is, indeed, the Trevithick Trail.

The next section, beyond Ann's Close in **Twynyrodyn**, provides the only routefinding difficulty. Go slightly uphill, then straight ahead into a no through road, which becomes Milbourne Close. The trail is then clearly signposted to the right, as a tarmac track heading into woodland. Very quickly, the site of Trevithick's famous tunnel is reached, although remarkably it is not well sign-posted from the trail, lying just to the west. ◄

The tunnel was 110m long and carried the tramroad directly beneath the calcining kilns of the Plymouth Ironworks.

Somewhat bizarrely, the trail briefly joins the dual carriageway coming down from Dowlais Top. Just beyond a roundabout, cross the dual carriageway and go through trees to emerge in a supermarket car park! Go right, then left between the store and a housing estate, and finally right again to rejoin the line of the tramroad as it runs between cricket pitches to the right and steeply rising farmland to the left.

One of the delights of the Trevithick Trail is the public art along the route, with one of the most strik-ing installations almost taking the form of a totem pole above **Pentrebach**. The trail lies well above the distant River Taff here, with superb views across to the Gethin Woodland Park on the far side of the valley. To the left is open wooded countryside, a favoured habitat for cuckoos from April onwards, while to the right a wooded bank provides an effective screen for the valley-floor housing and indus-trial units.

Suddenly, the trail enters the upper edge of the village of **Troedyrhiw**, keeping well above the village centre and heading along a sub-urban street for a while, before emerging just as quickly into wooded countryside. A council notice here asserts that dumping is not just pro-hibited, but 'absolutely prohibited'. The track now drops

Map continues on page 181

180

down to join the valley road. The tramroad went straight across here, since it can be seen below the road, with railway and river lower down still, but frustratingly this part of the historic route is inaccessible.

Eventually, the trail rejoins the route of the tramroad, shortly before a plaque at the mid-point of the route commemorating the opening of the Trevithick Trail. Beyond the river was the site of the Merthyr Vale colliery, while to the left the Garden of Remembrance for those who died in the Aberfan disaster in 1966 is clearly in view. The trail enters **Merthyr Vale** village on Tram Road (Tramffordd), heading south, with the railway to the right.

The trail parallels the railway for around 800m, then crosses it on a new footbridge

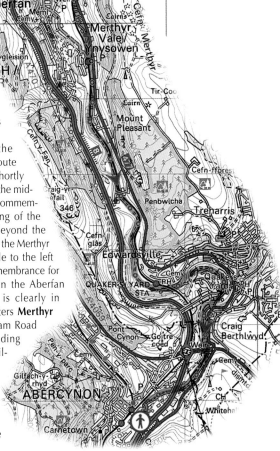

The reclaimed site of the Merthyr Vale colliery

– quite how the tramroad accomplished the crossing is unclear – and runs through woodland, with gravel suddenly replacing tarmac, and the stone sleepers that underpinned the tramroad clearly visible. The way lies through a cutting as the valley narrows and, for the first time, traffic noise from the A470 is faintly audible above the birdsong. Now the trail enters the Pontygwaith nature reserve, just before the magnificent bridge over the tramroad, high and steeply inclined, which carries an ancient trackway (now just a minor lane) down to and across the river.

It is very much worth a detour along this lane, passing Pontygwaith Farm and its tempting tea garden, to see the superb steeply arched river bridge, called Pontygwaith or 'bridge of the works', since it led to an early ironworks. Then climb back up to the tramroad, now also used by the Taff Trail, as it journeys south on a bench above the river, with the original stone sleepers again very prominent. ◄

Two sets of sleepers supported wooden rails, with the draught horses walking between the sleepers.

The journey through industrial history continues as the trail passes the remnants of two towering viaducts, their central spans long demolished but the remaining piers still evocative of the astonishing level of activity in this confined river gorge: these two long-vanished railway lines, the existing railway on a third viaduct a little down-stream, the Glamorganshire Canal and the tramroad all competed to carry the products of the Merthyr furnaces down to the coast at Cardiff and Newport.

Just below the surviving viaduct, the tramroad is forced to the west bank of the Taff for the first time, running through the gorge before returning to the east bank over a second bridge. ▸

Both bridges date from 1815 and replaced timber structures after the upper bridge collapsed while a tram was crossing the river.

A lane then takes the tramroad under two massive modern road viaducts to reach its southern terminus at **Abercynon** (originally called Navigation). The surviving Navigation House Inn was the headquarters of the canal company and the large area to its north formed a basin where goods from the tramroad were loaded onto barges, which crossed the river on an aqueduct and headed for the coast on the Glamorganshire Canal.

WALK 29

The Cistercian Way to the shrine at Penrhys

Start	The Old Bridge, Pontypridd (ST 073 904)
Finish	The shrine at Penrhys (ST 003 946)
Distance	9 miles (14km)
Ascent	565m (1850ft)
Time	4–6hrs
Map(s)	Explorer 166
Public transport	There are very frequent trains and buses from Cardiff to Pontypridd. Rail link bus 902 runs hourly from Penrhys to Ystrad Rhondda station (trains to Pontypridd and Cardiff).

A mere taster for the hugely ambitious 650-mile (1080km) Cistercian Way, this walk's destination is the historically important (if unlikely) religious site of Penrhys. In the 15th century, Penrhys was one of the most sacred places in Wales, with pilgrims flocking along routes such as that from Llantarnam Abbey to worship at the shrine of the Virgin Mary and seek cures for their afflictions in the healing waters of Ffynnon Fair (St Mary's Well).

Cross the Old Bridge, which lies at the north end of Pontypridd town centre, and take the tree-lined riverside Sion Street for the river view before doubling back, turning left into Fish Lane, left again into West Street and along The Parade through the suburban streets of **Trallwn**. Turn left and cross the River Taff again on a narrow road bridge (locally known as the White Bridge) just below the site of the old timber bridge, Pont-yr-Hesg. This was one of four timber bridges that spanned the Taff in the 16th century. It was described as decayed in 1580, probably because the dissolution of the monasteries meant that the monks at Llantarnam no longer provided for its maintenance.

Map continues on page 186

The Old Bridge is the most unlikely of triumphs – a spectacular bridge built by a self-taught mason, William Edwards, whose first three attempts collapsed, swept away by flood water. The fourth bridge, completed in 1756, was at that time the longest single arch bridge in Britain. It was constructed with three circular holes on each side to lessen the weight of the structure. Now used only as a footbridge, it retains its famously steep slope.

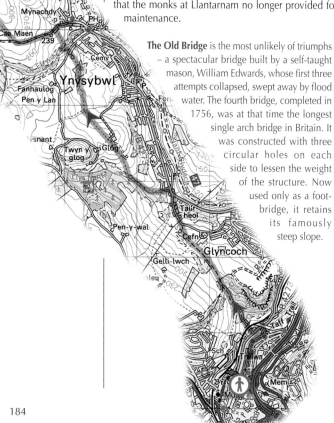

After crossing the White Bridge, turn left, then after 200m turn right into Darren Ddu Road, which narrows as it passes under a railway bridge and then climbs steadily to a barrier. Here the road disappears – its course now claimed by a stream – but a track climbs roughly parallel to the former road through the attractive woodland nature reserve of Coed Craig-yr-Hesg. At the top of the nature reserve the route continues along the narrow, undulating Darren-Ddu Road, a stony track forming a much degraded version of the old parish road from Pontypridd to Ynysybwl. The track is now fringed by semi-natural woodland as it drops down alongside a little stream to reach the main road to Ynysybwl.

Turn left along this road for just a few metres, and then left again into Brookfield. When this bends right, go straight ahead on a path that rises with a brook in a small gorge to its left. On the far side of the brook the remarkable remains of Ynysybwl's drift mine lie in thick undergrowth. The mine was a failed venture by the Great Western Mining Company, which drove a trial drift into the hillside but failed to find coal. Nearby is the massive Strawberry Wall, with a single archway intended as the principal entrance into the mine, and so-called because wild strawberries grew there.

The track rises steadily between the sprawling mining village of Ynysybwl and the altogether more rural **Twyn y glog**, a curious oval hill with a stone-walled ring cairn on a natural shelf near the summit. Leave the track well before Cribyn Du Farm, taking a path that runs through several fields and then a wooded copse. Keep ahead on leaving the woodland, passing a walled enclosure to the left and then going to the left of Bethel Cottage to find a flight of steps down to a minor road. Take a footpath slightly to the right, signposted to Llanwonno, descending to cross a little stream. Turn right along the far bank, and then climb away from the stream and cross a field to reach a rough track, with the substantial buildings of Mynachdy Farm across a small stream to the right. ▶

Turn left up the rough track, passing a barn and then a house on the left, and with increasingly good views

Mynachdy was a grange farm of Llantarnam Abbey, and doubtless provided shelter for those making the pilgrimage to the shrine at Penrhys.

Looking across the Taff Valley to Mynydd Eglwysilan

back over the Taff Valley to Mynydd Eglwysilan. The track rises steadily for some time, then levels off and reaches a gate with a choice of two routes. Take the right-hand track; Llanwonno Forest is now straight ahead. Eventually, the track enters the forest, making straight for the hamlet of **Llanwonno**, which consists of little more than a good pub (the Brynffynnon Arms) and St Gwynno Church, with

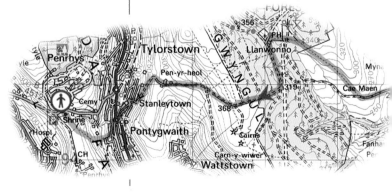

early medieval stone crosses and the grave of Guto Nyth Bran. ▶

Head south on the minor road from Llanwonno, then veer right onto a forest track that rises gently through recent clear-fell, which is now a good area to hear and sometimes see nightjars late on summer evenings. A path joins from the left; a little way along this are the medieval platform houses, clearance cairns and cultivation ridges of Carn-y-wiwer.

Beyond the gate at the edge of the forest there are completely different views to savour, as the Rhondda Fach comes into view ahead. Pilgrims saw Penrhys for the first time here. The green fields in the valley floor contrast with wooded slopes above classic terraced housing and the striking Tylorstown Tip, a local landmark, which now seems almost incongruous in an otherwise restored landscape. The track now begins a steep descent, sometimes on slabby bedrock, to the farmstead at Cefn-llechau-uchaf and, still further down, **Stanleytown** (where 80 terraced houses were built for £166 each in 1895 by the Stanley Building Society).

Guto was an exceptional runner in the 18th century, whose achievements are celebrated in the annual Nos Galan race on New Year's Eve in nearby Mountain Ash.

Classic terraced housing in the Rhondda Fach from above Stanleytown

Follow the road as it drops steeply to reach the main road at a roundabout. The Rhondda Fach River flows beneath the roundabout, on the site of Pont Gwaith-yr-Haearn, the Ironworks Bridge. Take the road signposted to Pontygwaith, cut up a lane to Madeline Street and take the footpath straight ahead. Turn right to reach a grassy track crossing the plateau on which the holy site of Penrhys is located, some distance away from the housing estate that has appropriated the name. A little below the statue of the Virgin Mary are the remains of Ffynnon Fair and the end of the walk.

The grange farm at **Penrhys** was owned by the Cistercian Abbey of Llantarnam, but became famous in medieval times for its chapel, shrine and holy well, Ffynnon Fair, which was reputed to have healing properties. The shrine, said to have miraculously appeared in an oak tree and comprising a statue of Jesus and his mother, was dismantled by royal decree in 1538, but Penrhys remains a place of pilgrimage for Catholics, who come to see the solid replacement statue, erected near the site of the chapel in 1953.

The statue of the Virgin Mary at Penrhys

WALK 30
Senghenydd Dyke

Start/Finish	Llanbradach station (ST 147 900)
Distance	8½ miles (14km)
Ascent	420m (1380ft)
Time	4–6hrs
Map(s)	Explorer 166
Public transport	There are four trains an hour from Caerphilly and Cardiff to Llanbradach.

This is a walk through history on the broad ridge between the Taff and Rhymney valleys. It takes in the substantial remains of a medieval deer park boundary marker, the Senghenydd Dyke; the Bronze Age round barrows of Carneddi Llwydion and Garnedd Lwyd, together with a prehistoric cairnfield, which seems to relate to farming practices rather than burials, and traces of cross dykes thrown up to impede unwanted passage along the ridgeway in early medieval times.

Just north of **Llanbradach** station, take the footpath that doubles back up the hillside, and climb steadily through bluebell woodland before crossing a stream. Turn right onto a clear track that eventually emerges above the trees; cross a sheep pasture, leave the track and cut diagonally left up a steep field to a broken stile. Keep to the hedge line across the next field to emerge on the broad ridge-top track, with the bank and ditch of Senghenydd Dyke already clearly visible 50m to the west.

> Medieval deer parks are common in England but a rarity in Wales. **Senghenydd Park** was the creation of the de Clare family of Caerphilly Castle. About a thousand hectares in size, it was the ultimate medieval status symbol and would have been stocked with deer and game, with a 7½-mile (12km) long bank and ditch. The bank was probably topped with a 'pale' or fence facing inwards to prevent the deer

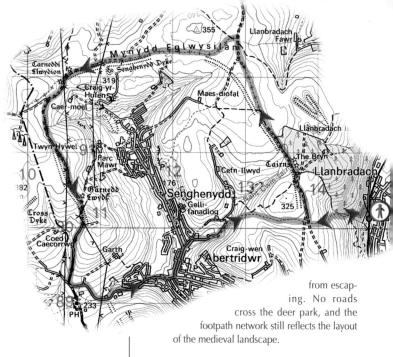

from escaping. No roads cross the deer park, and the footpath network still reflects the layout of the medieval landscape.

The broad, sandy ridge track drops slightly to cross the head of Cwm-Sarn, with Abertridwr down to the left. It then climbs up to the remarkably flat plateau of Waun Deliad, with the top of a forestry plantation and then the striking, serrated disused coal tips above Llanbradach Isaf to the right, and a fine section of the dyke to the left, with a double-banked ditch heading unerringly up the slope.

Ignore the first track turning left, but take the second, heading west across the southern slopes of **Mynydd Eglwysilan**, in the company of skylarks, meadow pipits and swallows, the latter hawking for insects in the close-cropped turf. The walking is easy on a rutted green track, with a wall coming up from the valley of the Glan Nant and then running alongside the track. The wall follows the line of the dyke and forms a prominent feature in the landscape for the next hour or more as the walk rounds the head of the Senghenydd Valley. On the western flanks

of Mynydd Eglwysilan is a group of six or so prehistoric cairns, lying on both sides of the dyke, which are reputed to be of agricultural origin, rather than being associated with burials.

The track detours to the right of the boundary wall for a while, joining the narrow mountain road between Senghenydd and Nelson and then going straight on across open moorland, where the road turns sharply left. The Rhymney Valley Ridgeway comes in from the right – the views northwards here of the upper Rhymney Valley, with the peaks of the Brecon Beacons a distant backdrop, are outstanding – and the track then passes the twin cairns of **Carneddi Llwydion**. ▶

The wall following the ancient line of Senghenydd Dyke comes up again from the left as the track curves gently left to cross the shoulder of Cefn Eglwysilan. The remains of three cross dykes designed to control passage along the ridgeway can be discerned to the right, and south of Twyn Hywel another excellent section of the dyke can be followed just to the west of the track. There are also good views into and across the Senghenydd

The wall marking the boundary of the deer park at the head of the Senghenydd Valley

Less impressive visually than historically, these round barrows have a central mound and a surrounding bank, but rise less than a metre above the surrounding moorland.

Valley on the left, with spoil heaps and quarries hinting at past industrialisation. The low mound of Garnedd Lwyd, just to the left where the stone wall leaves the track, is another round cairn, represented by low heaps of stones.

Follow the track downhill – the dyke crosses the track here and heads off to the left – and leave Eglwysilan Common at a gate; the route lies straight ahead down a narrow lane, still seemingly remote but actually remarkably close to the unseen Taff Valley. Eglwysilan church is strikingly in view ahead, with the Garth Mountain behind. The Rhymney Valley Ridgeway goes straight on at a crossroads, but the route lies left, taking a quiet country lane, which reaches the former mining settlement of **Abertridwr**.

Turn left by the disused Panteg Hotel. When the main road curves to the left, turn right into Bryn Gelli Terrace. It is a stiff climb to the top, where there is an inviting stile leading to a footpath across three fields and through a farmyard to a minor road. Turn left here, then right up a track that curves sharply right and contours above a shallow valley to the right. Beyond a gate the track trends downhill; leave it here, taking a narrow path half-left to reach a stile, with the ridge-top track used earlier in the walk now clearly in view ahead. Go straight across the track, reversing the outward route across three fields and through the woodland on the valley side to return to Llanbradach station.

The deer park in the upper Abertridwr Valley

WALK 31
Clydach Gorge south

Start/Finish	Clydach picnic site (SO 230 134)
Distance	5 miles (8km)
Ascent	280m (920ft)
Time	3–4hrs
Map(s)	Outdoor Leisure 13
Public transport	Bus X4 provides an hourly service between Cardiff and Abergavenny, stopping at the Clydach turn.

This is an intricate but richly rewarding walk that unravels the complex landscape of the Clydach Gorge, east of Brynmawr, and one to be savoured slowly. The steeply incised gorge of the Clydach River provides dramatic scenery and is of great natural interest, but also acts as the backdrop to a rich collection of archaeological and historical remains, including hillforts, quarries, ironworks and limeworks, and the densest network of surviving early tramroads anywhere in Wales. Not to be confused with the Clydach Valley north of Swansea, explored in Walk 1, this is a rather special heritage walk in sensational scenery.

From the picnic site, take the road through **Clydach** village, climbing steadily until, just above the ironworkers' terraced houses in Bath Row, the road bends sharply right, while a footpath signposted to Clydach station carries straight on up the hillside. The path runs through open beech and oak woodland, crossing a stream and rising steadily to the viaduct that carried Bailey's tramroad, later to become the Merthyr, Tredegar and Abergavenny railway, over Cwm Dyar.

The change in scenery on reaching the tramroad is dramatic. To the right are the overgrown platforms and old buildings of Clydach station, together with the former Station Hotel. Ahead, the scene is dominated by the remains of the Clydach limeworks and the adjacent Gilwern quarry. There are substantial remains of the limeworks, including two fine kilns with their double draw arches (built around 1877), a ball mill for making ground lime, and concrete aggregate bins fed from a crusher in Gilwern quarry.

The tramroad is signposted to Gellifelen station, but that will be visited later in the walk, so instead go to the left of the old station buildings and take a green track rising over a stile and between low banks across a field. There are superb views to the right of the Black Mountains, with the Iron Age hillfort known as Clydach Camp closer and to the left. The path bends left, passes through a farm and zigzags higher to become a track heading for the upland hamlet of Waunllapria.

Just before the Jolly Colliers pub, take the narrow lane to the left, climbing up to a delightful common with sensational views across the gorge to the limestone pavement on the slopes of Mynydd Pen-cyrn and back

Waunllapria common and the Sugar Loaf

to the Black Mountains and the distinctive Sugar Loaf Mountain.

The lane drops down past the pretty Mount Zion Methodist Church to the **Llam-march** crossroads. Keep straight on here (actually going right on the main road, and then left across a miniature gorge) and follow the quiet lane – its hedgerows alive with small birds including finches and warblers – around an incised valley and down to another offset crossroads.

> Constructed in 1821, **Bailey's tramroad** connected Crawshay Bailey's Ironworks at Nantyglo to the wharf at Govilon on the Brecknock and Abergavenny Canal. It was converted to a standard gauge railway in 1862, complete with tunnels where the tramroad turns were too difficult for rail wagons, but was never commercially prosperous and was closed in 1958.

Only 100m beyond the crossroads, a path leads under a pylon to a gate leading on to Bailey's tramroad, met for the second time in the walk. The tramroad, metalled in this section, runs past the remains of Gellifelen station to the western portals of the Gellifelen tunnels. It is possible – at your own risk! – to walk through the left-hand tunnel, but it is damp, dark, curved and 330m long, so many will regard it as more prudent to follow Bailey's tramroad round to the left, passing the path leading down to Devil's Bridge across the River Clydach and an abandoned cottage, before crossing a deep valley and, at the eastern entrance to the tunnels, swinging left on a shelf below sheer cliffs.

The tramroad, now a wide green track, occupies the left-hand half of the shelf. The right-hand half is now an extraordinary linear flower meadow, with bloody cranesbill, St John's wort and knapweed in abundance among a remarkably wide array of plants. The track swings sharply right below the cliffs, and then crosses Cwm Llam-march on a viaduct, now with the renowned Clydach nature reserve immediately on the left. The beech woodlands here are at virtually the western limit for beech in Britain; they flourish on the thin, stony soils of the steep valley sides.

Go straight across at a road (there was formerly a level crossing here) to view the dramatic **Llanelly quarry**, which provided flux for Clydach ironworks, immediately on the right, but then return to the road, follow it downhill for 100m and take a signed footpath on the left. The path drops down through the nature reserve to the Danycoed estate, running behind houses to reach the end of a cul-de-sac. Turn right here, passing bungalows built on a former slag heap from the ironworks, then go left along a road and further left still on a grassy incline, which leads directly to the ironworks.

> **Clydach ironworks**, whose surviving elements still dominate the local landscape, was opened before 1795, with four furnaces in operation half a century later. Financial losses were sustained during the 1840s and production ceased in 1861. The substantial remains of two large furnaces and

Clydach ironworks

the foundations of the associated casting houses, including an impressive archway, can still be seen.

At the far end of the ironworks site, a cast iron bridge dating back to 1824 takes the route over the River Clydach. Cross the river again after just a few steps, this time on a stone bridge, and take a path on the left that leads back to the picnic site.

WALK 32

The Iron Mountain Trail

Start/Finish	Rifle Green car park, Blaenavon (SO 251 094)
Distance	12 miles (19km)
Ascent	450m (1475ft)
Time	5–7hrs
Map(s)	Outdoor Leisure 13
Public transport	Bus X24 provides a service every 10 minutes between Newport and Blaenavon.

This sensational walk explores the extraordinary landscape of the Blaenavon world heritage site – one of a select group of sites chosen by UNESCO for their outstanding universal value, in this case because it bears 'eloquent and exceptional testimony to the pre-eminence of South Wales as the world's major producer of iron and coal in the 19th century'. The trail explores forges, quarries and the extensive remains of tramroads, inclines and water management features.

Start from the **Rifle Green** car park in Blaenavon (the 'official' starting point for the trail is Keeper's Pond but this is remote from public transport). Cross the Brynmawr road and follow Stable Row for 100m, before turning right onto a signposted footpath that gives a sudden, astonishing bird's-eye view of the Blaenavon ironworks. The path crosses a stile and joins the Brynmawr road. Keep on the road until, opposite a bus stop, a signposted track

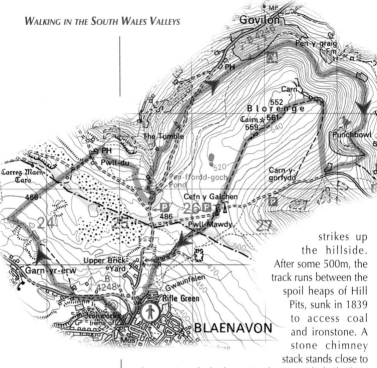

strikes up the hillside. After some 500m, the track runs between the spoil heaps of Hill Pits, sunk in 1839 to access coal and ironstone. A stone chimney stack stands close to the remains of a brake engine house, with the braking machinery in a stone-lined pit, at the top of the tramroad that connected the pit to the ironworks.

One of the best-preserved examples of its type in the world, **Blaenavon ironworks** was constructed from 1787 onwards. The complex is dominated by an impressive water balance tower, which raised pig iron processed in the ironworks 25m for export along the tramroads. There are also extensive remains of one of the original blast furnaces and two more built to meet increased demand during the French wars; the cast house, where molten metal was shaped into ingots or 'pigs'; the foundry, where it was wrought into finished products; and terraces of workers' housing in Stack Square.

Bear slightly left on passing the chimney, then right onto the roughly surfaced Dyne-Steel Incline. This double-inclined standard gauge railway, constructed in the 1850s by Thomas Dyne-Steel, deputy manager of the ironworks, took pig iron from the ironworks to the Garnddyrys forge (visited later in the walk). Now, it provides an arrow-straight way across the flanks of Cefn Garnyrerw. At the summit of the incline, the low walls of the engineer's cottage and the winding house for the incline can be seen. It then trends downhill as a roughly-surfaced track, concreted during the 1940s to facilitate opencast coal mining as part of the war effort. ▸

As the slope eases, the trail reaches the remains of the village of **Pwll-du**. The former welfare hall, now an adventure centre, and the Lamb and Fox pub are the sole remaining buildings. Yet, in 1851, there were chapels, a school and a shop. Opposite the adventure centre lies one of the stone-arched western entrances to the Pwll-du tramroad tunnel, the longest horse-drawn tramroad tunnel ever constructed in Britain.

18th-century workers' housing at Stack Square

The Canada Tips on the right, named after the Canadian troops who supervised their operation, are the only first-generation opencast mines to survive.

The trail leaves the tramroad, which becomes overgrown here, and runs to the right of the pub in the direction of the Blorenge Mountain. Eventually, it leads onto the stone-walled embankment of a former pond, created to power the operation of a balance lift that moved wagons up and down a vertical shaft cut into the face of Pwll-du quarry, which lies to the left of the trail. Turn right at the end of the balance pond to reach **Pen-ffordd-goch Pond** (locally known as Keeper's Pond). The pond was the highest of three reservoirs supplying the forge at Garnddyrys, and has sensational views across the Usk Valley to the Sugar Loaf Mountain and the limestone escarpment of Pen Cerrig-calch.

Walk along the left side of the pond, then cross the B4246 – once the Abergavenny to Blaenavon turnpike road – and take a path curving around the east side of Cwm Ifor, then down the old parish road of Rhiw Ifor to its junction with Hill's tramroad. Turn right, walking along the tramroad as it contours along the hillside, and then follow the well-signposted path through the extraordinary remains of the Garnddyrys Foundry.

> **Garnddyrys** converted pig iron from Blaenavon ironworks, producing 300 tonnes of wrought iron bars and rails a month in its pudding furnaces and rolling mills. Stone-walled former reservoirs, huge misshapen lumps of reddish-brown slag, and the lines of tramroads entering the site hint at its former importance.

From Garnddyrys, follow the orange waymarks through a walled enclosure containing further remains – now reduced to brick rubble and low stone walls – of the village of Garn Ddyrys Row and the scanty remains of the Queen Victoria pub as the route rejoins Hill's tramroad, now a green track contouring the steep north face of Blorenge Mountain. The tramroad connected Blaenavon ironworks with Garnddyrys and Llanfoist Wharf on the Monmouthshire and Brecon Canal. Some of the original stone tramroad sleepers can still be seen, together with a cut-and-cover tunnel and the marshalling yard where the wagons were manoeuvred from the tramroad for their descent down the Llanfoist incline to the canal basin below.

The path continues around the mountain, above Llanfoist Wood, and enters the Coed Cadw/Woodland Trust nature reserve, centred on the **Punchbowl**, with its brown, reed-fringed pool in a glacial hollow gouged from the side of the mountain. Blue dragonflies flit above the pool in summer, with green woodpeckers in and around the stand of trees at the far end of the pool, their curious yaffling call common in spring and early summer.

Leave the Punchbowl to the south, climbing quite steeply up a delightful track wedged between an ancient stone wall to the left and the mountain slopes to the right. The track climbs gently to a bench, with a superb view north of the Skirrid Fawr, its dramatic profile resulting from a landslip. Follow the green track to a gate to leave the nature reserve, and emerge at a complex junction of roads and paths. Turn right here, on a waymarked path climbing alongside a walled and wooded enclosure, gaining height steadily as the path makes its way through the heather to emerge on the summit plateau of the **Blorenge**.

> The open, windswept moorland of the **Blorenge** is home to many of the more common upland species, but the special bird of this mountain, attracted by the vast areas of undisturbed heather, is the red grouse. Plump and reddish-brown, the bird has a low, direct flight when disturbed, and a croaking alarm call; the impression is almost that of a chicken hurtling away from danger. Red grouse are rarely seen close to the paths that criss-cross the mountain, but can occasionally be flushed from nearby heather.

The thin path now threads its way across the peaty heather moor to the summit of the Blorenge; at 561m (1840ft) it is the highest point of the walk. The views are

Heather moorland on the summit slopes of the Blorenge

spectacular, although with a huge contrast between the post-industrial moorland landscape to the south-west and the pristine mountains to the north and north-west. The way forward is now obvious, along a springy, peaty track towards two TV masts. Just before reaching the masts, turn right to reach the Foxhunter memorial, commemorating the exploits of the Olympic gold-medal winning show jumper owned by Sir Harry Llewellyn. Foxhunter is buried here, and when he died in 1999, Sir Harry's ashes were scattered nearby.

A path skirts the pond of **Pwll Mawdy**, where the landscape reflects the way in which it was 'scoured' with water in a primitive attempt to flush out the iron ore outcropping close to the surface. Traces of ponds, scours, adit mines, leats and yet more tramroads can still be discovered. The track descends to reach Ball's Pond reservoir and emerges on Elgam Road. Cross the road, follow the stepped path downhill and continue straight ahead to reach Broad Street and the centre of **Blaenavon**. The town itself is well worth exploring, with colourful terraces, chapels and churches (including St Peter's, built by the ironmasters with many cast iron items) and the Big Pit mining museum.

APPENDIX A
Route summary table

No	Title	Distance	Ascent	Time	Map(s)	Page
1	Cwm Clydach and the Swansea Canal	8 miles (13km)	200m (655ft)	3–4hrs	Explorer 165	30
2	Along the Tawe Valley	5½ miles (9km)	Negligible	2–3hrs	Explorer 165	34
3	The Cwm Cregan Trail	6 miles (10km)	150m (490ft)	2–3hrs	Explorer 166	39
4	The Taff Trail	15 miles (24km)	220m (720ft)	6–8hrs	Explorer 151, 166	42
5	Along the Monmouthshire and Brecon Canal	11 miles (18km)	Negligible	4–5hrs	Explorer 152, Outdoor Leisure 13	48
6	The Usk Valley Walk	12 miles (19km)	150m (490ft)	5–7hrs	Explorer 152, Outdoor Leisure 13	53
7	Mynydd Garn-Fach and the upper Lliw Valley	7½ miles (12km)	260m (855ft)	3–4hrs	Explorer 165	60
8	The Gnoll, Melincourt Falls and the Neath Canal	12 miles (19km)	330m (1080ft)	4–6hrs	Explorer 165 (small section on 166)	64
9	The Coed Morgannwg Way	27½ miles (44km)	1315m (4310ft)		Explorer 166 (small section on 165)	68
	Stage 1	14½ miles (23km)	775m (2540ft)	6–9hrs		69
	Stage 2	13 miles (21km)	540m (1770ft)	6–8hrs		74
10	Between the Llynfi and Garw	9½ miles (15km)	560m (1840ft)	4–6hrs	Explorer 166	79

No	Title	Distance	Ascent	Time	Map(s)	Page
11	The Glamorgan Ridgeway	27 miles (43km)	1515m (4970ft)		Explorer 151, 165, 166	84
	Stage 1	10 miles (16km)	520m (1705ft)	4–5hrs		86
	Stage 2	8 miles (13km)	350m (1150ft)	6–8hrs		91
	Stage 3	9 miles (14km)	645m (2115ft)	4–6hrs		95
12	Over the Bwlch	10 miles (16km)	385m (1260ft)	4–5hrs	Explorer 166	101
13	The Rhymney Valley Ridgeway	8 miles (13km)	180m (590ft)	3–4hrs	Explorer 151, 152, 166	105
14	Above the upper Rhymney	13 miles (21km)	465m (1525ft)	5–7hrs	Explorer 166, Outdoor Leisure 13	109
15	The Sirhowy Valley	8 miles (13km)	235m (770ft)	3–4hrs	Outdoor Leisure 13, Explorer 166	115
16	Mynydd Carn-y-Cefn and the Round Towers	5½ miles (9km)	420m (1380ft)	3–4hrs	Explorer 166, Outdoor Leisure 13	119
17	St Illtyd's and the Guardian of the Valleys	10 miles (16km)	470m (1540ft)	4–6hrs	Explorer 152, Outdoor Leisure 13	123
18	The Raven Walk	12 miles (19km)	920m (3020ft)	6–8hrs	Explorer 152, 166	128
19	High Folly and packhorse trails	8 miles (13km)	375m (1230ft)	4–6hrs	Explorer 152, Outdoor Leisure 13	133
20	The buried town of Kenfig	7 miles (11km)	Negligible	3–4hrs	Explorer 151/165	139
21	Ewenny Priory and Merthyr Mawr Warren	9 miles (14km)	220m (720ft)	4–5hrs	Explorer 151	143

No	Title	Distance	Ascent	Time	Map(s)	Page
22	Castles around Cowbridge	7 miles (11km)	170m (560ft)	3–4hrs	Explorer 151	148
23	The Glamorgan Heritage Coast	10 miles (16km)	390m (1280ft)	4–6hrs	Explorer 151	152
24	The Border Vale	9 miles (14km)	210m (690ft)	4–6hrs	Explorer 151	158
25	Deserted villages and folk museum	9 miles (14km)	330m (1080ft)	4–6hrs	Explorer 151	162
26	St Illtyd's Walk in upland Gower	14½ miles (23km)	540m (1770ft)	6–8hrs	Explorer 165 (small sections on Explorer 178 and Outdoor Leisure 12)	168
27	Sarn Helen	9 miles (14km)	250m (820ft)	4–6hrs	Outdoor Leisure 12, Explorer 165 (small section on Explorer 166)	174
28	The Trevithick Trail	9½ miles (15km)	Negligible	4–5hrs	Explorer 166	179
29	The Cistercian Way to the shrine at Penrhys	9 miles (14km)	565m (1850ft)	4–6hrs	Explorer 166	183
30	Senghenydd Dyke	8½ miles (14km)	420m (1380ft)	4–6hrs	Explorer 166	189
31	Clydach Gorge south	5 miles (8km)	280m (920ft)	3–4hrs	Outdoor Leisure 13	193
32	The Iron Mountain Trail	12 miles (19km)	450m (1475ft)	5–7hrs	Outdoor Leisure 13	197

APPENDIX B
Useful contacts

Public transport

There is an excellent network of public transport services providing access to almost all towns and villages in the South Wales valleys, with many of these services running surprisingly frequently. Information on train services can be found at www.arriva trainswales.co.uk or by calling 08457 484 940 (or 08456 040 500 for information in the Welsh language). Traveline Cymru (www.traveline-cymru.info or 08712 002 233) offers comprehensive bus timetable information, but it is sometimes easier to access timetables via the relevant local authority website (see below).

Accommodation

The first port of call for information should be Visit Wales (www.visit-wales.co.uk or 08708 300 306) which has details of a wide range of possibilities in all price ranges, from hostels and bed-and-breakfasts to good-quality hotels. In addition, notes on accommodation options for the two multi-stage walks in this guide (Walks 9 and 11) are given in the introductory text for those walks.

Tourist information centres

A number of tourist information centres are strategically located in south Wales and are able to offer detailed advice on public transport, accommodation, maps and leaflets for the local area. Among the most useful are those at Blaenavon (01495 742333), Bridgend (01656 654906), Caerphilly (029 2088 0011), Cardiff (029 2087 3573), Merthyr Tydfil (01685 727474), Porthcawl (01656 786639) and Swansea (01792 468321).

Local authorities

All the local authorities in the area have websites with substantial amounts of information relating to tourism, recreation and transport in their area; the most important are those for:

Blaenau Gwent (www.blaenau-gwent.gov.uk),
Bridgend (www.bridgend.gov.uk),
Caerphilly (www.caerphilly.gov.uk),
Cardiff (www.cardiff.gov.uk),
Merthyr Tydfil (www.merthyr.gov.uk),
Monmouthshire (www.monmouthshire.gov.uk),
Neath Port Talbot (www.npt.gov.uk),
Newport (www.newport.gov.uk),
Rhondda Cynon Taf (www.rctcbc.gov.uk),
Swansea (www.swansea.gov.uk),
Vale of Glamorgan (www.valeofglamorgan.gov.uk).

CICERONE GUIDES TO THE BRITISH ISLES

For full information on all our guides, and to order books and eBooks, visit our website:
www.cicerone.co.uk.

Walking – Trekking – Mountaineering – Climbing – Cycling

Over 40 years, Cicerone have built up an outstanding collection of 300 guides, inspiring all sorts of amazing adventures.

Every guide comes from extensive exploration and research by our expert authors, all with a passion for their subjects. They are frequently praised, endorsed and used by clubs, instructors and outdoor organisations.

All our titles can now be bought as **e-books** and many as iPad and Kindle files and we will continue to make all our guides available for these and many other devices.

Our website shows any **new information** we've received since a book was published. Please do let us know if you find anything has changed, so that we can pass on the latest details. On our **website** you'll also find some great ideas and lots of information, including sample chapters, contents lists, reviews, articles and a photo gallery.

It's easy to keep in touch with what's going on at Cicerone, by getting our monthly **free e-newsletter**, which is full of offers, competitions, up-to-date information and topical articles. You can subscribe on our home page and also follow us on **Facebook** and **Twitter**, as well as our **blog**.

Cicerone – the very best guides for exploring the world.

CICERONE

2 Police Square Milnthorpe Cumbria LA7 7PY
Tel: 015395 62069 info@cicerone.co.uk
www.cicerone.co.uk